With sports being more [...] with sports unifying peop[...] [...]kgrounds and beliefs, with sports—let's face it—being a religion to many men, *In the Arena* could not have come at a better time. Christians and non-Christians alike need to know what sports really are. Sports are more than exercise, more than Xs and Os, more than competition. David Prince examines the depth of this wonderful gift of God with a thorough, insightful, and biblically sound treatment that will not only deepen your understanding of sports but also your understanding of the God who created them.

Chris Broussard, award-winning journalist for ESPN, author, founder of The K.I.N.G. Christian Men's Movement, and on-air NBA thought leader (ESPN, ABC)

There is no one on the planet I would rather read on a theology of sports than David Prince. Prince is a preacher of the Word and a lover of sports. This book is perfect for athletes, for coaches, for parents, and for pastors. The book shows how to love Jesus and love sports without idolatry or a sour spirit. This is a book filled with wisdom, truth, and joy. David Prince applies the gospel to the playing field and knocks it out of the park.

Russell Moore, president, Southern Baptist Ethics & Religious Liberty Commission

As a former NFL Player, now pastor, I've been waiting for someone to write this book! That someone is David Prince. With *In the Arena*, David teaches us that sports is a gift of God, a manifestation of cultural rootedness, a competitive manifestation of the performing arts, an opportunity for worship, a testing ground that exposes character, and an opportunity for witness. This book is so good. This book is a guide for parents and the athletes they love.

Derwin L. Gray, lead pastor,
Transformation Church and author
of *Limitless Life: You Are More Than
Your Past When God Holds Your Future*

While some Christians uncritically absorb sports and others withdraw altogether, David Prince strikes the right balance: sports are meant to be good but are never ultimate. Sports are a "nonessential but inevitable" activity of people made in God's image. David Prince has given followers of Jesus a resource that is richly theological and intensely practical, equipping the reader to enjoy sports as a gift from God for the glory of God.

Jeremy Treat, Reality L.A., pastor of Preaching and
Vision, adjunct professor of Biola University

With so many Christians discussing various matters related to faith and culture, it is a bit surprising to find so few books addressing faith and sports—for this subject plays a huge role in cultures around the world. I often get questions about how one should view athletics as a Christian. As a former college baseball player, I used to ask some of these same questions. So I am glad Prince has tackled this subject biblically, theologically, and practically. I appreciate his content and his clear writing style. He hit a home run with *In the Arena*! I recommend it not only for those involved in sports, but also for everyone who lives in a culture surrounded by sports.

Tony Merida, lead pastor, Imago Dei Church
and associate professor of Preaching
at Southeastern Baptist Theological Seminary

The world of sports seems to be on trial for Christian parents as our family priorities are being placed in a false dichotomy with our children's participation in sports or even our adult enjoyment as fans of the teams of our youth. This is a timely book from David Prince—a father, pastor, professor, and sports enthusiast. The enjoyment of sports by Christians is something that needs to be reclaimed and redeemed, and as a father and sports fan myself, I am thankful for David Prince's treatment of such an underrated area of discipleship for all of us who love to enjoy athletics. Sports are part of our sanctification, and Prince rightly and uniquely points us to this truth.

Dean Inserra, pastor, City Church Tallahassee

David Prince is a husband, father, pastor, sports enthusiast, and my personal friend. He is ideally suited to speak to the issue of sports, home, and church and frankly is saying things to which every family should listen. Every mom, dad, and pastor should buy this book. In fact, I think every pastor should buy this book for every mom and dad in his church. That's how important I think it is.

Randy Stinson, Ph.D., senior vice president
for Academic Administration and provost at
The Southern Baptist Theological Seminary

Sports are a wonderful gift from God—but, as with every good gift, sports can become perverted into a god. In this book David Prince leads you on a theologically grounded, Christ-centered journey that will enable you and your family to enjoy the gift of sports without letting it become your god. Highly recommended!

Timothy Paul Jones, C. Edwin Gheens
Professor of Christian Family Ministry at
The Southern Baptist Theological Seminary
and author of *The Family Ministry Field Guide*

It is a strange irony that American Evangelicals spend so much time following and practicing sports, but such little time thinking through the ramifications. That is why I am so grateful for David Prince and his fine book, *In the Arena*. In this book Prince brings a robustly biblical argument to bear about the commendability of sports, sacrifice, discipline, and the pursuit of excellence for the glory of God.

Jason K. Allen, president,
Midwestern Baptist Theological Seminary

I have known David Prince since he was nineteen years old. To say that he is a sports enthusiast is to completely understate the obvious. But serving first as his pastor and now a co-laborer in ministry, I can also attest that Christ is ultimate in his life, not sports. Parents and families in our sports-dominated culture need the message of this book for many reasons; but finding the skill and wisdom to balance sports and Christian development tops the list. As David says so beautifully, sports can (should!) actually be a primary means for Christian training. Sports can be idolatrous for many, but *In the Arena* will help root out such false thinking and elevate the goodness of God in all things. God is ultimate and sports can serve to show Him that way. You should read this book and gift it to many.

Greg Belser, pastor,
Morrison Heights Baptist Church

I have spent most of my life on a baseball field either competing as a player or as a coach in the rugged Southeastern Conference for twenty-six years. It is refreshing and encouraging to read a biblical perspective on something I have loved for so many years. Thanks to David Prince, I see my passion and chosen vocation more as a gift from God. Thanks for master-fully articulating both the challenges and blessings for people who love sports.

Keith Madison, former baseball coach at the University of Kentucky, national baseball director for SCORE International, and publisher for *Inside Pitch* magazine

Christian sports fans know that sports can be good and edifying, but also that there are lines that can be crossed at which point devotion to sports becomes sinful. Who can help us think through these issues? You may not know David Prince, but I do. And if I were asked to pick one person I could trust to write about sports from a biblically sound, theologically informed, God-centered, church-based, family-oriented, eternally minded way, David Prince would be one of the first three names that would come to mind. So whether you are a Christian who enjoys sports or a believer who questions the value of athletics, this quickly read book will challenge you with biblical thinking on the subject.

Donald S. Whitney, professor of Biblical Spirituality, The Southern Baptist Theological Seminary and author of *Spiritual Disciplines for the Christian Life*

IN THE
ARENA

IN THE
ARENA

THE PROMISE OF
SPORTS FOR CHRISTIAN
DISCIPLESHIP

DAVID E. PRINCE

PUBLISHING GROUP

NASHVILLE, TENNESSEE

To my wife Judi with whom, by God's grace, I have the privilege to share all things. Without your Christ-honoring example, love, support, and encouragement this book would never have been written. May God grant us many more years together, may those years include many more trips to the ballpark, and an Atlanta Braves world championship.

Also, to my children:
Luke
Will
JP
Lydia Grace
Susannah Faith
Sarah Hope
Phoebe Joy
AnnaBeth Mercy

I cannot believe I have the privilege of you calling me dad. I pray that you will always courageously be *In the Arena* for Christ and lead your children to do the same. May you, like an athlete, exercise "self-control" any time you seek to win a "crown that will fade away," but may it always be with a single-minded focus to honor Jesus, who alone graciously provides "a crown that will never fade away" (1 Cor. 9:25).

Acknowledgments

In some sense, I've been preparing to write this book my entire life. I was born into a sports family and grew up in a city, Montgomery, Alabama, that is sports crazy. My dad, Julian Prince, spent countless hours investing in me becoming the best ballplayer and person that I could become. His example is one I have attempted to replicate with my children. I regret that my mother, Blanche Prince, did not live to see this book published. She loved me unconditionally, and I can't fathom how many hours she spent sitting in the bleachers and working in concession stands as I competed in sports. My sister, Julie Burns, was a better athlete than I during our childhood, which made me work all the harder. Her present encouragement in my life is a constant blessing.

Every coach I ever played for, every person I competed against and with at the National League (Dixie Youth Baseball), Capitol Heights Junior High School, Robert E. Lee High School, George C. Wallace Community College, and Huntington College has indirectly contributed to this book. My coaching stops at Saint James High School and McAdory High School have helped shape this book as well. While I mention a few of these important people in the book, there are far more people to thank in the span of years than I could write here. Please know that I am thankful for my hometown, home state, and all of the people the providence of God has afforded me the privilege to meet and who have shaped my life.

Much of my thinking for this book was sharpened and clarified in pieces about sports and Christianity I have had the privilege to write for the Ethics and Religious Liberty Commission of the Southern Baptist Convention. The president of the Ethics and Religious Liberty Commission, Russell Moore, has been a constant encourager, friend, and teacher in my life for more than two decades. Everything I do and think has been impacted by his Christ-centered theological genius and passion. Also, lectures on sports and Christianity that I gave at The Southern Baptist Theological Seminary where I am honored to serve as an assistant professor of Christian Preaching produced ideas that have been developed in this book. The conversations that followed those lectures has helped me immensely, and I am thankful for each person who took the time to engage me on this topic.

I also want to thank my friend and colleague at The Southern Baptist Theological Seminary, Provost Randy Stinson. We share a love of Jesus and a delight in the national pastime. We have been talking about Jesus, the gospel, church, husbanding, child-rearing, and baseball for more than two decades, and I am a better man in every area because of his wisdom and friendship. The pastors I serve with at Ashland Avenue Baptist Church—Jeremy Haskins, Nate BeVier, and Casey McCall—are a happy band of gospel warriors who see my writing ministry as important enough to bear greater burdens so I can pursue projects like this. Jeremy Haskins consistently challenges me in ways that strengthen me as a follower of Christ. Casey McCall was a voluntary editor of this volume and his suggestions improved the final product. Ashland Avenue Baptist Church members Zac Lewis and Hannah Shultz, brilliant young scholars, also read the manuscript and provided excellent suggestions and insights.

B&H Publishing Group has been an absolute delight to work with on this project. Toby Jennings was my editor as the project began and made many helpful suggestions for which I am thankful. Devin Maddox worked with me at the conclusion of the project. The book project began at Devin Maddox's urging and his professionalism, wisdom, creativity, and thoughtfulness have been a blessing. He also has the good sense to cheer for the Atlanta Braves, which was a bonus. No book is an individual project no matter whose name is on the cover, and that is especially true of this one. B&H Publishing Group strives for Christ-centered excellence, and I am grateful to work with them.

The book is dedicated to my wife Judi and our eight children. To merely say "thank you" to them is woefully inadequate. Each of them has sacrificed so this book could be written. Judi is quiet and strong, a helper fit for me, who teaches me about the kingdom of Christ daily, as I watch her love and serve our family and others. To Judi I say, I love you, I enjoy you, and I cannot imagine life without you. Thank you for loving and encouraging me, and for every midnight load of laundry to get red clay out of baseball pants, grass stains out of football pants, and to get tennis outfits ready for the next day so our children could compete. And thank you for being committed to using sports as a tool to point them to Christ and to teach them to follow Christ. To my children, I want nothing more for your life than for you to be courageously *In the Arena* for Christ and his kingdom, spending and being spent, for the sake of the gospel.

Contents

Introduction: In the Arena 1

CHAPTER ONE: Sports Matter 13

CHAPTER TWO: Sports and Fandom 29

CHAPTER THREE: Sports and Spiritual Warfare 47

CHAPTER FOUR: Sports and Christian Discipleship 65

CHAPTER FIVE: Sports and Self-Esteem 85

CHAPTER SIX: Sports and Safety 101

CHAPTER SEVEN: Sports and the Church 117

Conclusion 139

Notes 145

Introduction

In the Arena

"It is not the critic who counts; not the man who points out how the strong man stumbles, or where the doer of deeds could have done them better. The credit belongs to the man who is actually in the arena, whose face is marred by dust and sweat and blood; who strives valiantly; who errs, who comes short again and again, because there is no effort without error and shortcoming; but who does actually strive to do the deeds; who knows great enthusiasms, the great devotions; who spends himself in a worthy cause; who at the best knows in the end the triumph of high achievement, and who at the worst, if he fails, at least fails while daring greatly, so that his place shall never be with those cold and timid souls who neither know victory nor defeat."

Theodore Roosevelt[1]

President Theodore Roosevelt was a zealous sports fan. He defended football from its critics, urged youth to be involved in sports, and even regularly boxed in the White House when he was the president of the United States. In one sparring bout, a crushing punch to Roosevelt's left eye resulted in a detached retina and blindness (a fact that he kept as a guarded secret). His doctors ordered him to stop boxing, so he immediately took up jujitsu instead. In a letter to his son attending college, he wrote, "I am delighted to have you play football. I believe in rough, manly sports." But he also added an important qualifier, "Athletic proficiency is a mighty good servant, and like so many other good servants, a mighty bad master."[2]

The "In the Arena" quote from Roosevelt's "Citizenship in a Republic" speech has long been a favorite of mine. The speech emphasizes Roosevelt's belief that the success of a republic rests not so much on the brilliance of its citizens as on the disciplined and courageous work and character of its citizens. Roosevelt tenaciously believed that one learned best by doing, and that it is better to stumble and fail than to do nothing or to sit by and criticize those who are "in the arena" striving and doing. The man worthy of praise is the one who willingly fights honest battles even if those battles end in defeat. Sideline cynicism and aloof critical detachment are the ways of cowardice and shame. Roosevelt believed sports were culturally valuable because they put people in the arena and provided limited but authentic tests of character.

It is understandable that many athletes have drawn inspiration from Roosevelt's "Citizenship in a Republic" speech and, particularly, the statement that has simply come to be known as the "In the Arena" quote. NBA star LeBron James has the quote posted on his locker and references it often as his favorite quote. Before the 1995 World Cup, Nelson Mandela gave a copy of the passage to Francois Pienaar, captain of the South African rugby team, and they won, defeating a heavily favored team from New Zealand.[3] Former Washington Nationals' utility player Mark DeRosa would read the quote to himself before games; when the Nationals faced the St. Louis Cardinals in Game 4 of the National League Division Series in 2012, DeRosa read it aloud to his teammates.[4]

Roosevelt's call to action echoes what we find in Scripture. God calls his people to be fully engaged, Christ-centered participants, not spectators, in the arena of life. Christians know the greatest enthusiasms, the greatest devotions, and spend themselves in the worthiest cause—the spread of the gospel. As the apostle Paul declares, "For to me to live is Christ, and to die is gain" (Phil. 1:21). In another letter the same apostle writes, "I will most gladly spend and be spent for your souls" (2 Cor. 12:15), and is quoted elsewhere, "For I am ready not only to be imprisoned but even to die in Jerusalem for the name of the Lord Jesus" (Acts 21:13). When everything is said and done, our greatest regrets will be the risks we didn't take. What Roger Angell said of baseball could be applied in some measure to all athletic competition: "Baseball seems to have been invented solely for the purpose of explaining all other things in life."[5]

God is sovereignly directing the course of redemptive history, and he graciously writes his people into the script that he has provided us in the divine gospel drama of Scripture. God has placed us in the arena of his world, and we are to play our parts by living for his glory no matter what comes our way. God kindly provides us the windows of smaller arenas where we can be challenged to demonstrate the virtues necessary for faithfulness in the ultimate arena of our lives before God, our Creator and Sustainer. The Bible offers athletic competition as one of those windows; it is a biblical metaphor with which many people today have the most direct experiential contact. The smaller arena of sports is one way we can have our physical and moral courage tested. Sports provide limited and temporal consequences with the pressure of success and failure. Athletic competition provides practice games for life, whether experienced by participation or observation, but to benefit fully, we must be intentional about the lessons it can teach us.

I am thankful athletic competition has always been a part of my life. When I was younger, I certainly corrupted the gift of athletics by treating it as an ultimate end rather than an opportunity to worship the God who alone is ultimate. Nevertheless, the problem was with my sinful and idolatrous heart, not with sports. My father was teaching me about sports before I could walk. One photo of me as an infant shows a ball right beside me in the crib. My parents bought the house in which I was raised partly because it was across the street from baseball fields, a football field, and a basketball court. The smaller sporting arenas of my childhood and young adulthood will always be sacred places to me. I rarely travel to my hometown of Montgomery, Alabama, without driving by Joe Marshall Baseball Field where I played baseball as a child, the East YMCA where I played football and basketball, Paterson Field where I played high school baseball, and Huntington College where I played college baseball.

As a Christian husband and father, one of my great joys has been to share my love of sports with my wife, Judi, and our eight children. Judi and I met in college, and she knew absolutely nothing about baseball. Now, she loves baseball almost as much as I do. After I taught her to keep a baseball scorebook, the first game she ever scored herself came on July 28, 1994, when Kenny Rogers of the Texas Rangers pitched only the fourteenth perfect game in Major League Baseball history at the time. When I am away from home and unable to watch our beloved Atlanta Braves, she keeps me updated with text messages about how the game is going.

As I write this, my oldest son, Luke, is a freshman in college. Not long ago he was home and recounted his favorite sports memory. He competed at the varsity level in baseball, football, and track during high school, but his favorite memory was when he was twelve years old playing on a baseball team I coached along with Will, his then eleven-year-old brother. We started out as the worst team in the league but had steadily improved. We were playing in the postseason tournament as the last seed but had made it to the championship game. Leading by one run going into the final inning, the team who had finished the regular season in first place loaded the bases with no outs. We pulled the infield in to get the force-out at home plate, and somehow our infielders knocked down two consecutive sizzlers and threw home for the first two outs. There was one out standing between us and the championship, so we moved the infield back because we could get the final force-out at any base. They hit a dribbler that made it past the pitcher, and Will, playing second base, scooped it up with his momentum going toward the plate and fired home to get the final out by the slimmest of margins. From worst in the regular season to first in the postseason tournament, those boys felt like they had won the World Series. Something tells me they will be recounting and remembering that night for the rest of their lives.

In recent years, I have also become a tennis dad. Tennis is a sport in which I only dabbled as a child, but now several of my children play competitively. I have grown to love the sport because of the sportsmanship inherent in the game and the fact that it is uniquely grueling and mentally taxing. My second oldest son, Will, says that while he has played baseball, football, and basketball, tennis is the most mentally challenging of them all. My oldest daughter, Lydia Grace, plays competitively, and my favorite match she ever played was one that she lost when she was twelve years old. It was a championship match against a very good opponent, and my daughter's serve was torturously bad to begin the match. She lost the first set handily, and her opponent's father began creating drama by yelling and arguing. To make matters worse, she started the second set by breaking a string on the only racket she had. We had to find her another racket to use, and she lost a point because of the delay. Things looked bleak, but she began to battle and won the second set. The match went to a ten-point tiebreaker, and she took an early lead but ended up losing 11–9 in the tiebreaker. I told her after the match that I was kind of glad she lost; I didn't want her to think that my delight in her tenacity and ability to overcome obstacles was due to her winning.

I could continue recounting stories like these for the entirety of this book, but I will not. Both of the events that I just explained have led to countless conversations about what it means to follow Christ and to serve his church. They are reference points, lessons learned in smaller arenas, that have profound implications when thinking about the ultimate arena of life. My purpose in this book is twofold. First, I will examine sports from a biblical-theological perspective. Second, I will practically examine how sports provide a limited but genuine window that can help us apply our lives to the gospel story revealed in Scripture. I desire for this book to be a valuable resource in helping Christian coaches and players on all levels, from youth leagues to professional, as well as in assisting parents of athletes and fans in thinking biblically and intentionally as Christians about their participation in and enjoyment of sports. Along the way we will keep in mind Theodore Roosevelt's helpful admonition, "I trust I need not add that in defending athletics I would not for one moment be understood as excusing that perversion of athletics which would make it the end of life instead of merely a means in life."[6]

Most of my illustrations and concrete examples related to sports will involve baseball, football, and basketball. The simple reason for this is that, growing up in Alabama, these were the sports of my childhood. Sports are a manifestation of our cultural rootedness, and my roots are in the soil of the Deep South. Simply put, I love the sports that my father loved and taught me. Nevertheless, I think the principles contained in the illustrations are equally applicable to the sports that you love and enjoy. I like to joke with my friends that

the sports I like are superior to the sports they like, but
I actually think the cultural diversity illustrated by the
variety of sports, like the cultural diversity of music and
art, is a manifestation of the expanse of God's glory.

In chapter 1, we will attempt to develop a basic biblical theology of sports and competition. This chapter
is foundational for the conclusions drawn in the rest
of the book. Anyone who wishes to participate in and
enjoy sports from a distinctively Christian perspective
must seek to understand where sports fit in the world
that God created and where sports fit in the lives of
his image bearers. What should Christians think about
sports? Are sports a distraction and waste of time for
Christians? Is competition biblically justifiable? Can
sports be a way to worship and serve God? This chapter
will address these questions.

Chapter 2 will focus on fandom. There are some
who might think that participation in sports is valuable
because of the lessons it provides to the participant but
that the experience of simply being a spectator and fan
of sports is a waste of time. In this chapter, we will
think about sports in relation to a theology of humanity, place, and cultural rootedness. This chapter contends that neither withdrawal from sports or uncritical
absorption of sports culture is a distinctively Christian
response and will call Christians to a cruciform engagement with sports.

In chapter 3, we will examine the relationship
between sports and spiritual warfare. Anyone engaged
in sports as a participant or fan will immediately notice
the prevalence of military language. Why is the apostle
Paul fond of both military and athletic metaphors for
Christian living? What are the distinctive biblical

lessons Christians are to glean from athletic competition? This chapter will seek to answer these questions while also providing warnings about how Christians sometimes abuse the Bible and the language of their faith in relation to sports. This chapter will also help to identify when sports have become an idol displacing God rather than a means of honoring God.

Chapter 4 examines the usefulness of sports for Christian discipleship. In what ways do sports provide a helpful metaphor for the Christian life? How can we approach sports in light of the supremacy of Christ? Do sports build character as many people often suggest? What are some general guidelines for parents who want to prioritize Christian discipleship as their children participate in sports? How should Christian parents approach training their child when he or she is sitting the bench on their sports team? This chapter will seek to answer these questions and also deal with the danger of detaching youth sports from parents by over-professionalizing them.

In chapter 5, we will consider sports and the modern self-esteem movement. This chapter will argue that the contemporary trend toward not keeping score under the belief that "everybody is always a winner" actually works against what makes sports a valuable biblical metaphor and tool for cultivating Christian character and virtue. This chapter will also provide Christian parents with some basic guidelines for a distinctively Christian approach to utilizing sports involvement in cultivating a biblical, gospel-centered worldview that contends against our narcissistic culture.

Chapter 6 will address the issue of sports and safety. It will seek to answer some of the cultural opposition

to physical and rough sports. It will show that rough
sports have always had cultural critics. Is it safe for
Christians to adopt a "safety at all costs" mentality? Is
football too dangerous? Is a world where people believe
nothing is more important than personal safety worth
living in? If the Bible teaches self-sacrificial courage as
a virtue but refers to self-referential safety as a vice,
how should that reality inform our attitude about sports
involvement? This chapter will seek to answer these
questions as it explores the relationship between sports
and teaching the virtue of self-sacrificial Christian
courage.

Chapter 7 examines the relationship between sports
and the church. The primary focus of this chapter will
be the ways in which sports can provide lessons that
are helpful and applicable to our lives as accountable
members of local churches. I will discuss my experience
as an unbelieving high school baseball player learning
the beauty of sacrifice in the game of baseball from a
Christian coach who was dying of cancer. We will also
look at how I believe my time as a high school football
coach uniquely prepared me for the challenges of day-
to-day life as a pastor of a local church. This chapter
will also discuss the historical examples provided by
Branch Rickey and Jackie Robinson of Christian moral
courage in Major League Baseball and what those two
ferocious Christian gentlemen can teach the church as
we serve Jesus together in our daily lives.

The book concludes with some simple guidelines
for Christians as they participate in and enjoy sports.
While I believe there is benefit in reading the book in
order from beginning to end, the chapters have been
constructed so that they can serve as stand-alone

chapters as well. The person who desires to flip to a chapter of interest will be able to benefit from doing so without having to read the rest of the book. Some repetitiveness has been retained for the benefit of those who wish to read a chapter of interest independent of the rest of the book.

Chapter One

Sports Matter

*And whatever you do, in word or deed, do
everything in the name of the Lord Jesus,
giving thanks to God the Father through him.*

(Colossians 3:17)

Sweating profusely, I felt like I might become physically ill. It was January 1, 1979, and Alabama was playing Penn State in the Sugar Bowl. I was ten years old and Penn State was about ten inches from the goal line at the end of the fourth quarter. A touchdown and an extra point by the Nittany Lions would tie the game and put hopes of a national championship in jeopardy for my beloved Crimson Tide. Over twenty-five years later, I still get butterflies in my stomach when I think about watching that moment. I was on my hands and knees as Penn State handed the ball to fullback Mike Guman, who attempted to leap into the end zone ten inches from the goal line. Alabama linebacker Barry Krauss, like a fullback-seeking missile, met Guman over the top and stopped him in his tracks. My family went berserk with cheers and hugs. The play is simply known in Alabama football lore as "*The* Goal Line Stand."

I can also recall countless memories from my days competing in sports, from coaching high school athletics, and now from coaching my own children. My children often recount every minute detail of games they have competed in as well. At any moment, my mind can be transported back to those scenes, recalling them with dramatic detail as if they were happening right now in slow motion. Some of those memories are of jubilant victories and others of painful defeats. I played on a very talented high school baseball team where many players, including myself, went on to play college baseball. It was a fantastic experience, but I still cannot get over the fact we never beat our crosstown rival, Jefferson Davis High School. During my senior season, they were our play-off opponent, and we carried a 3–0 lead into the late innings only to lose 4–3. The bitter pain of walking off that field is still with me today, and I continue to have an aversion to the green and gold of our heated rival's school colors.

Why do sports affect so many of us in this way? Why does athletic competition touch something deep within us and sear us with profound memories that leave vivid imprints on our hearts and minds? Why do so many of us spend time following and cheering for our favorite teams? Why do we organize our schedules to get our children to and from practices? Why do we sit in the stands in the heat and the cold to watch them compete? Is it simply a matter of misplaced priorities and wasting our lives on trivial pursuits as many Christians often imply?

After giving a talk on sports and Christian disciple-ship in a seminary setting, a professor approached me and said, "We don't need sports to accomplish our Christian gospel mission, so why would we care?" It is a sentiment I have frequently encountered among some evangelical Christians. I responded by asking him, "Do you read books other than the Bible, theology, and com-mentaries? Why?"

In the Beginning . . . Creation and Sports

It is true that sports are not fundamentally neces-sary for human survival but neither are singing, danc-ing, reading novels, hiking, or strolls on the beach. Sports may not be necessary, but they are an inevitable and reflexive response to the world God created. Our love of sport reveals something of our identity as people uniquely created in the image of God. Song is not neces-sary to human sustenance and existence; nevertheless, singing is an instinctive and appropriate response to God's creative work. Such is true of all of the perform-ing arts, of which sports are a competitive manifesta-tion. God did not create sports—people did. But people created sports in response to the world God created. Sporting competition is capable of reflecting God's cre-ative glory and design in his image bearers, and thus presents an opportunity to celebrate our unique iden-tity in God's world.

If direct gospel ministry and Bible reading are all that matter, then we waste most of our lives in the meaningless daily stuff of ordinary living. What are sports? The answer is simple: sports are a manifesta-tion of culture. Andy Crouch (following Ken Myers) has helpfully summarized culture as, "what we make of the world" God has created and the meaning we assign to it.[1] A spirituality that does not meet us in the daily root-edness of workplaces, ball games, and house cleaning is sub-Christian. This ought to be evident to the followers of the Word, who "became flesh and dwelt among us" (John 1:14).

What are some evidences of culture? From the podium at which I preached Sunday, to the clothes I wore, to things like ballet, drama, gardening, cooking, music, literature, hunting, and building—these are all manifestations of culture. Too often, some Christians self-righteously denounce popular manifestations of culture, like sports, as a waste of time with no self-awareness that they themselves participate in and enjoy a variety of cultural manifestations. Song, art, construction, creation, and competition are reflexive cultural responses to the glory of our Creator God.

The idea that passion for God should make us pas-sionless for other cultural things like sports is suffocat-ing to our worship and deadly to our gospel mission. God calls his followers to live comprehensively distinc-tive lives in particular places and at particular times in history. The theological commitments of those who follow Jesus as King are to be lived out daily and geo-graphically. God's image bearers dwelling in particu-lar places will inevitably build, draw, sing, play, and compete. Christian distinctiveness should be evident in the corporate gospel activities and ministries of a local church, and it must also be evident as the church scat-ters to live as salt and light in every single area of life, including the athletic field.

The Work of Dominion and Double Plays

Sports provide us spectacular glimpses of truth, beauty, and goodness as athletes tune and discipline their bodies to perform amazing feats of skill, coordination, choreography, and strength. I have never understood why some who fancy themselves champions of *the arts* look down their noses at sports and athletic competition. Playing the violin or cello is a skilled and glorious feat that should be applauded, but I personally happen to think few things in the world are as beautiful and majestic as a well-turned 6-4-3 double play, and I make no apologies for it. In fact, when I witness the smooth beauty of a double play, I sense a pale reflection of the beauty and glory of God.

Answering the question of why so many of us love sports takes us back to the very beginning. According to his good pleasure, God created the world out of nothing (Gen. 1): "By faith we understand that the universe was created by God's command, so that what is seen has been made from things that are not visible" (Heb. 11:3 HCSB). God's creative command produced an original world without precursor. God declares that the power of his creative word produced a created world that he described as "good" (Gen. 1:4, 12, 18, 21, 25), and he described his creation of human beings in his own image as "very good" (Gen. 1:31). God is the only One who can create out of nothing, but as we make and shape necessary and nonessential things out of what God has made (culture making), we are capable of reflecting the truth, beauty, and goodness of our Creator God.

Man was uniquely created in the image of God, and as such, he was created to work and rule the world under the authority of God: "Fill the earth, and subdue it. Rule the fish of the sea, the birds of the sky, and every creature that crawls on the earth" (Gen. 1:28 HCSB). This command to rule is often referred to as the cultural or dominion mandate and reveals that worshipping and glorifying God is an active pursuit and not a passive one. God glories and delights in his creative work and calls for his image bearers to do the same in innumerable ways.

The unique responsibility of humanity involves the glory and honor of ruling God's earthly kingdom-creation under his authority as expressed in his Word (Gen. 1:26–28; 2:19–20; Ps. 8). In so doing, humanity will glorify and delight in God's creative work by working to shape what he has made into things that glorify him and prove good for his image bearers (Gen. 2:15–25). In order to accomplish the work of dominion, human beings have to develop, hone, and maximize their God-given abilities in submission to the Creator. Such honing can only be done through actively and aggressively exercising the gifts God provides his image bearers for the purpose of subduing and filling the earth to the glory of God. This work of honing our culture-making skills would inevitably include all sorts of competition, including sporting competition.

Redemption: Eating, Drinking, and Sports to the Glory of God

Adam and Eve's rebellious disobedience to God's word pervasively corrupted God's good creation. God responded by pronouncing curses (Gen. 3:14, 17) and judgment (Gen. 3:16–19). God is later described as "grieved" (Gen. 6:6) in regard to the corruption of his creation. Body, mind, and soul were holistically marred by the fall into sin and are in need of redemption. The tragic events that disrupted the harmony of the entire created order, including the shame and alienation of man and woman in the presence of God, would not be the final word; God's grace would be (Gen. 3:15). It is possible that Jesus began his conversation with the weary disciples on the road to Emmaus (Luke 24) with the gospel promise of Genesis 3:15. The Bible can rightly be understood as a series of extended explanations of how the prophetic word of promise in Genesis 3:15 of Christ's final victory over the serpent unfolds in redemptive history as Jesus makes "all things new" (Rev. 21:5). Thus, the redeeming work of Christ extends to church, home, workplace, informal play, and formal sports.

The entire biblical story line follows the ongoing cosmic war between the kingdom of God in Christ and the parasitic kingdom of the serpent. The pattern of biblical history is often helpfully summarized in its broadest patterns as creation, fall, redemption, and new creation. The center of the conflict is Jesus as "the Word," in whom "all the promises of God find their Yes" (Gen. 3:15; John 1:1–14; 2 Cor. 1:20). Christ is the promised seed, the fulfillment of Genesis 3:15. The Great Commission explains how the cosmic warfare of the gospel promise of Genesis 3:15 centers on Christ and unfolds in the new covenant as his followers go into all the world in his name and make disciples (Matt. 28:16–20). Living for Christ as faithful gospel warriors means an earthy, real-world, embodied spirituality that pervades every aspect of culture in order to redeem it. Athletic contests, particularly in team sports, bear remarkable similarities to military battle, so the connection and shared metaphors between sporting competition, warfare, and spiritual warfare are readily apparent.

Biblically, we must understand that spiritual warfare is not merely a specialized ministry for select individuals. Spiritual warfare is what it means to follow Christ in a fallen world. It is all-encompassing and touches every area of our lives. The book of Revelation's description of the eschatological (ultimate) triumph of the kingdom of Christ and the final defeat of "that ancient serpent, who is called the devil and Satan" (Rev. 12:9) represents the full and final vindication of the textual Word of God (Rev. 22:16–21) and Christ, the personal Word of God (Rev. 19:13; 20:4). As the redeemed followers of Christ live in the "already" of Christ's kingdom and await the "not yet" of his final kingdom consummation, we are to reclaim *all aspects of creational life* for the kingdom of Christ. Living faithfully for Christ as our King is not simply a matter of a few big spiritual moments. It means that every single aspect of our lives must be surrendered to him. As some sports teams like to say, it is a matter of being *all in, all the time.* Scripture makes no attempt to sever the connection between the lesser and nonessential agony and conflict of sports from the ultimate and eternally significant agony and conflict of spiritual war.

The gospel is the gospel of the kingdom of God in Christ. God is at work redeeming his image bearers and ultimately the entire created order. Thus, nothing matters more than the kingdom of God in Christ, but we must also say with equal fervency that because of the kingdom of God in Christ, everything matters. Exercising dominion to the glory of God in a fallen world calls for more than utilitarian work and activity. Acting as though only directly religious activities really matter would render far more than sports as meaningless. Viewing the world in that way would constitute a refusal to delight comprehensively in God's creative work and design. In other words, we must avoid the futile tendency to separate the world into religious (sacred) and nonreligious (secular) spheres. The responsibility of glorifying God in a fallen world does not amount to a reductionist attempt to minimize the number of activities in life that *really matter*. Paul captures the corrective for this mind-set when he asserts, "Therefore, whether you eat or drink, or whatever you do, do everything for God's glory" (1 Cor. 10:31 HCSB).

Creation, people, place, and history are not spiritual problems; they provide the strategic setting for us to make much of Christ in our daily lives. Our hope is not found in escaping our body or this world for some abstract utopian spirituality, but in living every bit of our real-world lives to the glory of God in Christ. The story of your life is uniquely situated in a community of people at a particular place in the world. In Christ, the story of our lives is woven into the story of Christ to the degree that we are to be his witnesses wherever we are. Our real-world flesh-and-bone existence in some place on the world map is our providentially given strategic opportunity to live for Christ. The writer of Proverbs urges us to see the link between the rooted, daily pleasures of our real-world lives and delighting in

God, "My son, eat honey, for it is good, and the drippings of the honeycomb are sweet to your taste," because he explains, "Know that wisdom is such to your soul" (Prov. 24:13–14). This is similar to the way Paul persistently calls followers of Christ to link their interest in athletic competition to their ultimate calling, the battle to live for Christ in their daily lives.

God gave his image bearers intricately complex bodies that are "remarkably and wonderfully made" (Ps. 139:14 HCSB) and capable of amazing feats of strength, balance, running, jumping, and throwing. The desire to hone and maximize those gifts and to delight in those with exceptional abilities in doing so is a natural response to the glory of the Creator God and his redeeming work in a fallen world. Many Christians fail rightly to appreciate sporting competition because they wrongly assume that competition inevitably leads to sin or is an inherently sinful manifestation of the fall into sin. It is common to hear Christians say things like, "There cannot be sports in heaven because someone would have to lose, and no one will ever lose in heaven because it will be perfect." In the words of Lee Corso, "Not so fast, my friend!"

The Creator, Creature, and Competition

It is true that, in a fallen world, maintaining a proper perspective on competition and the result of winning or losing is difficult, but this challenge is not unique to sporting competition (think of education, business, and politics). The cultural mandate to rule the world under the authority of God came prior to the fall into sin and is a call to live aggressively for the glory of God. God calls his image bearers to strive together, overcoming obstacles and cultivating their gifts and abilities for communal good and for God's glory. This activity necessarily involves order, structure, and a competitive spurring along of one another to maximize our God-given abilities. Andrew Fuller (1754–1815), commenting on God's good gift of activity and work in the world (Gen. 2:15), wrote, "Man was not made to be idle. All things are full of labour: it is a stupid notion that happiness consists in slothful ease, or in having nothing to do."[2]

Our activity of shaping the good world that God created out of nothing into things that are useful is necessary to glorify God, but our work of cultivating things that are not functionally necessary but produce a sense of wonder and delight is also a foundational way we reflect God's creative glory in the world. Thus, things like the performing arts, of which sports are a competitive manifestation, while not compulsory, are nonetheless the indirect result of the design of God. Duty and delight are both means of exercising dominion in the world and serving under the authority of God (Luke 10:38–42). Rightly understood, both utilitarian and nonessential competition are good gifts of God for human flourishing because the goal is not to diminish the opponent but to help him or her cultivate their skills to the highest degree. In other words, rightly ordered competition is a means of considering one another and spurring one another on to glorify God.

Gather a group of children together to play and almost invariably they will begin to compete. One child will look at the other and say something like, "Let's see who can throw the ball against the wall and catch it the most times." The enjoyment of play and the resultant delight in competition is a celebration of the goodness of our creator God. Such joyful play points beyond itself to kingdom consummation in the Messiah's reign as Zechariah prophesies: "And the streets of the city shall be full of boys and girls playing in its streets" (Zech. 8:5). Informal play with minimal rules is the foundation of all formal sporting activity. Play turns into athletics and sports when the rules, boundaries, and goals of play are formalized into agreed-upon methods and restrictions.

One's sporting opponent provides the necessary resistance to expose weaknesses, which provides an opportunity for growth and betterment. It is the drama of competition that brings out the best in each side that makes sports so exciting and interesting. A sports league where all of the contests are lopsided would draw little interest from spectators. Thus, any "win-at-all-costs" or "winning-is-the-only-thing-that-matters" attitude in regard to sports is a corruption of God's good gift. But what is often forgotten is that participation in sports does demand a desire to win because that is the only way that the ingenuity, creativity, and effort of the competitive performing art can be drawn out and delighted in by participants and spectators.

Coaches and athletes often speak of the importance of a competitive spirit, and Christians should understand the vital nature of this kind of competitive spirit surrendered to the lordship of Christ. After all, life in a fallen world is difficult for all people, and a spiritual battle is raging. Every Christian has a responsibility to engage in the battle. There are eternal winners and losers in life. Proverbs 27:17 asserts, "Iron sharpens iron, and one man sharpens another," and as Duane Garrett writes, "[this verse] explains that people must not shy away from interaction with their peers since it is an education in itself. The 'sharpening' can occur in any area in which people are engaged, be it business, intellectual, or physical competition."[3]

The notion that there cannot be any sports in the new heavens and new earth because someone would have to lose is misguided on a couple of fronts. First, it presupposes that competition is inherently sinful or at least leads to sin. Honorable competition can spur creativity, focus, accountability, and the mutual sharpening of gifts and abilities. There is good reason that someone wanting to get in better shape often finds a friend with a similar goal to compete against in the gym. Similarly the government does not allow certain business monopolies because they often lead to a lessening of quality and taking advantage of the consumer. This is what we call healthy competition. Second, it suggests that losing a contest necessarily diminishes one's joy. On a practical level we know this is not true. When athletes are asked at the end of their careers what games they remember and cherish, they almost invariably bring up the most difficult ones or even the ones in which they were on the losing end. They will say something like, "It was such a joy to compete against such an amazing and gifted opponent." The biblical witness regarding competition is that respectful competition among those who recognize one another as fellow image bearers can be a celebrative activity that enriches lives and provides opportunity to glorify God.

Competition, rightly understood and ordered, is not simply about the individual competing; it is about the God who created him and the opportunity to be challenged to greater achievement because we live in community with other image bearers. Thus, the appropriate way to compete in sporting activities is to fight self-sacrificially to win the contest with all of your might, but having done so, to respect and admire your opponent for having done the same. In other words, the Christian should understand that his or her opponent is not the enemy; he or she is a friend whom God has provided to help him or her grow and develop and to cultivate God-magnifying excellence. The Christ-honoring competitor will be more competitive—not less. Nevertheless, the Christ-honoring competitor will not get his or her identity and self-worth from his or her performance because to do so would turn God's gift into an idol. Christian competitors thank God for the ability to compete, but they also thank God for their opponent's ability as well.

One example of a rightly ordered approach to competition at the highest level is Andrew Luck, quarterback of the Indianapolis Colts. Kevin Clark of the *Wall Street Journal* wrote an article noting that Luck has "become famous for congratulating—sincerely and enthusiastically—any player to hit him hard. Any sack is met with a hearty congratulation, such as 'great job' or 'what a hit!'" The article asked teammates why they think Luck responds by congratulating opponents for excellent plays, even ones where he is the direct victim, and they said the primary reason "was his sincere respect for a good play—even one that resulted in him getting knocked off his feet." One even said, "[if] Luck himself makes a great play, he usually says nothing—no matter the situation." His father, a former NFL quarterback himself, explained by saying, "We attempted to raise him with appropriate values, with respect for other people and to be kind and generous, and I guess that carried over to the football field."[4]

To God Be the Glory

Like all other areas of our lives, our understanding of competition and management of competitive desire is adversely affected by the fact that we are sinners. Some fuel their competitive desire by hating their opponents and desiring to harm them. Others come to sports with a self-referential, "winning-is-the-only-thing" mentality. These corruptions of the creational design of competition are no reason for Christians to withdraw from sporting competition; rather, they present an opportunity to reclaim competition for the glory of Christ and his kingdom. Sporting competition can provide a limited but genuine opportunity to honor God and love one's neighbor.

There is joy in pushing one's body to the limit in pursuit of an agreed-upon goal. There is communal delight in performing as part of a team in pursuit of victory or in celebrating a favorite team's victory in a culturally rooted sport of a particular geographical region. I am from Alabama, and you do not have to love the intricacies of the game of football to be swept up into the excitement of Friday night lights or Saturday afternoons at the local colleges.

There is a proper sense of awe that comes from seeing one of God's image bearers discipline and utilize his or her physical gifts in exceptional ways. For many of us, sports touch something deep within us and provide us a measure of pleasure, delight, awe, and wonder. Charles

Simeon's famous quote gets it right: "There are but two lessons for Christians to learn: the one is, to enjoy God in everything; the other is, to enjoy everything in God."[5] We should not be ashamed of the joy we find in sports. Rather, we should say, "To God be the glory!"

Chapter Two

Sports and Fandom

"In the same way, let your light shine before
others, so that they may see your good works
and give glory to your Father who is in heaven."

(Matthew 5:16)

Whenever I hear someone say, "War Eagle," or see someone wearing Auburn sports gear, I almost reflexively feel obligated to respond, "Roll Tide!" In fact, it seems like a duty—a moral responsibility even. Years ago, Bill Clinton's campaign guru and LSU alum, James Carville, was asked by the *Wall Street Journal* to explain the fanatical devotion of legions of fans who never took a step inside a classroom at the schools they follow. He quipped, "Half the people in that stadium can't spell LSU. It doesn't matter. They identify with it. It's culturally such a big deal."[1]

As a son of Alabama, the Heart of Dixie and the buckle of the SEC football belt, I would suggest this is one of those rare occasions when James Carville was understated. To call football in the South "culturally . . . a big deal" is akin to saying the Grand Canyon is a big hole. I'm writing this chapter a short time after rivalry weekend in college football. Michigan and Ohio State meet each year in a historic border clash that is one of the greatest rivalries in all of sports. But when you hail from Alabama, rivalry weekend means only one thing—the Iron Bowl.

Anytime Alabama and Auburn meet on the football field, everything else in the state grinds to a halt. The 2013 Iron Bowl is now simply known as the Kick Six game; prior to the game it was hyped as the biggest ever and the miraculous ending lived up to it (though the wrong team won). Tickets with a face value of $95 were going for an average of $638 on the resale market. To put that in perspective, the state's average monthly mortgage payment was $809 in 2013. Football analyst Beano Cook once said, "Alabama-Auburn is not just a rivalry. It's Gettysburg South." The thought of a wedding or funeral in the state of Alabama on the day of the Iron Bowl would be met with a, "Bless their heart" and, "I'm sorry, I won't be able to make it." Even those who do not care about football and the outcome of any game on the gridiron are still unavoidably affected by the Alabama-Auburn rivalry because almost everybody else cares.

Wayne Flynt, professor emeritus in the Department of History at Auburn University, suggests that the South's devotion to college football is rooted in regional pride associated with the attempt to recover from the post-Reconstruction era. He notes that when Alabama headed to the 1926 Rose Bowl as a laughable opponent against the heavily favored Washington Huskies, the president of rival Auburn sent a telegram telling them, "You are defending the honor of the South, and God's not gonna let you lose this game."[2] Flynt also quotes the Vanderbilt coach saying, "Alabama was our representative fighting against the world. I fought, bled, died, and was resurrected with the Crimson Tide."[3] William J. Baker writes that after Alabama's victory, "Southern partisans joined in a kind of regional hallelujah chorus."[4] The stunning Alabama victory was immortalized in the school's fight song as fans continue to sing, "Remember the Rose Bowl, we'll win then. Go, roll to victory, Hit your stride, You're Dixie's football pride, Crimson Tide, Roll Tide, Roll Tide!"

In the southeastern United States, football has taken on a mythic quality. Auburn University's institutional school creed written in 1943 contains a focal reference to the priority of sports at the school: "I believe in a sound mind, in a sound body and a spirit that is not afraid, and in clean sports that develop these qualities." Football Saturdays in the South are not just games; they are cultural events similar to a massive family reunion. The pageantry and rootedness of cheering for the local school with which you identify is a contemporary reflection of southern agrarian rootedness. Flynt writes, "Football offered southern men a chance to assert their masculinity and the South's physical supremacy short of actually taking up arms."[5] The regional rootedness of football in the South is still on display as Southeastern football fans often chant, "S-E-C, S-E-C, S-E-C," when a Southeastern Conference school triumphs over a school from another region, and it also helps explain the South's preference for college sports over professional sports.

Sports and the Priority of Place

Baseball will always be my favorite sport, but as a son of Alabama, football certainly holds a special place in my affections. I naturally tend to write about the sports I know and love, but my observations should not be considered as exclusive to those sports. Sports reflect our sense of place and rootedness in the world God has made. The diversity of sports, sporting experiences, and preferences are a reflection of the providence and wisdom of God. The world is enriched by the diversity of music and art in various geographical locales around the world, and the same is true of the variety of sports. Like many Americans, I love baseball, football, and basketball, but people from other regions around the globe speak with similar delight about the sports that are rooted in their cultural identity: soccer, hockey, cricket, rugby, and so on. I am an unabashed fan of sports, but I do not write this chapter primarily as a fan; rather, I write as a Christian pastor and seminary professor. This discussion of sports fandom begs the question: Is the fanaticism good or bad? My answer is an unequivocal "Yes!"—it all depends on whether sports are summed up in Christ or abstracted from him.

As Flynt notes about football in the South, there is a sense in which affinity group allegiance to a particular sports team, especially when geographically based, is simply a cultural manifestation of the importance of place and rootedness. Our transient, globalized culture often feels awkward about our rootedness, but we must remember that when the cosmic Lord came in human flesh, he was known, even by demons, as "Jesus of Nazareth" (Mark 1:24). Some saw his rootedness in an ordinary family and a modest town as a liability (John 1:46; 6:42; 7:27). But Jesus was from somewhere, and it mattered. The same is true for us.

Our rootedness in this fallen world should serve our longing for rootedness in the world to come (Heb. 11:16). We have already had the opportunity to experience such gifts as family, fellowship, camaraderie, love, and place, however imperfectly. To act as though we come from nowhere is a prideful commentary on our understanding of the past as well as on our thoughts about the future. We all long to be a part of a community—an entity greater than the individual and one that helps to provide a sense of belonging, identity, and unity. These longings are meant to lead us to seek ultimate fulfillment in the only place it can be found: Jesus Christ and his unshakable kingdom community, the church. Nevertheless, it is most natural that these longings be reflected in other limited but genuine ways in our lives. When Christians live daily as the salt of the earth and the light of the world (Matt. 5:13–14), our Christian theology intersects with our geography and cultural interests, and we are then liberated in our daily lives to echo and embody the supremacy of Christ in all things (Col. 1:17–18; Eph. 1:10).

Rootedness is an important quality for our children as well. Many years ago at a pastors' conference I attended, someone asked pastor and theologian Sinclair Ferguson to share one piece of advice about parenting. His response, as best I can remember it, was something like, "Based on who is in this room, I would suggest you tie more than one string to your children. Teach them about God, teach them the Bible, but also have other interests with them as well. If you are into sports, then connect with them through sports. If you're into construction, then connect with them through construction. Use those interests to connect with them, and teach them about God through those as well." His admonition has always stuck with me. I would guess that his comments reflected a failure he had witnessed among pastors and seminarians to teach their children to sum up *all things* in Christ (Eph. 1:10).

In many ways sports fandom and team loyalty is a lot like patriotism for one's country. To despise one's nation is an act of rebellion against the providence of God, but blindly to idolize it is an act of rebellion of another sort. Patriotism, rightly understood in a Christian worldview, is a natural recognition of God's good providence and his sovereignty in determining our place, rootedness, and story. We come from somewhere, and we are part of a family line whose sacrifices in generations past have shaped our story. Our country and our families are not ultimate, but they are important. Showing them honor is a way we honor Christ (1 Pet. 2:13–17). The rootedness of sports is evident in cultural choices of sporting passions; metropolitan urban areas in the United States tend to enthusiastically embrace a professional sports team that is identified with a particular large city, whereas more rural areas tend to identify primarily with college athletics and state or regional universities.

Football, Fandom, and Humanity

The rootedness of our sporting passion helps keep Christians from dehumanizing those for whom we cheer as they compete—or at least it should. It has become fashionable among some to denounce collision sports in general, but football specifically, as barbaric and gladiatorial. Author Malcolm Gladwell has repeatedly called for colleges to drop their college football teams and has asserted that it is barbarism akin to dog fighting.[6] Roger I. Abrams, professor of Law at Northeastern University, asks regarding football, "Should we accept this gladiatorial combat as our national pastime?"[7] Such critics must be watching a different game than the one so many of us enjoy and look forward to each weekend in the fall. The overheated banal critiques of Gladwell and Abrams seem rooted in predetermined opposition rather than compelling and persuasive argumentation.

Far from being an example of barbaric gladiatorial culture, I think the beautiful and awe-inspiring controlled aggression of football is a cultural expression of the value of humanity, and it demonstrates an excellent example of the wonder and beauty of human spirit and passion. Rodney Stark has written that Christianity gained influence and spread so rapidly, in part, precisely because it countered the blood thirst of the gladiatorial culture: "Perhaps, above all else, Christianity brought a new conception of humanity to a world saturated with capricious cruelty and the vicarious love of death. . . . Finally, what Christianity gave to its converts was nothing less than their humanity."[8]

In a separate interview, Stark contrasts the violent culture of the gladiatorial games with what happens on a football field:

> If you look at the Roman world, you have to question whether half the people had any humanity. Going to the arena to enjoy watching people

tortured and killed doesn't strike me as healthy. I'm a big football fan, and I see that, when some player gets hurt, they bring out an ambulance and the doctors take twenty minutes to get him off the field. They don't want people hurt out there. But these people did. They'd shout, "Shake him! Jump up and down on him!"[9]

Modern American football is not a contemporary expression of a gladiatorial culture thirsty for gratuitous violence; it is the repudiation of it. Football is a potentially violent sport, but the point of football is not violence or the injury of the opponent. As Herm Edwards famously declared, "You play to win the game." Football games are won with power and finesse. It is a physically demanding collision sport that will certainly result in occasional injuries, some of which will be serious. But over the years, football has been willing to reform in countless ways in order to make it safer without destroying the essence of the manly, physically demanding game. Football does not reward coaches and players who corrupt the game by attempting to intentionally injure an opponent; it penalizes them.

As a former high school football coach, I have sadly witnessed players injured on the field and have consistently seen players on the opposing team show concern and even gather and pray for the injured athlete. Now, as a father, having watched my own son play high school football, I have observed the same recognition of humanity on the football field. I have been in Bryant-Denny Stadium with 100,000 rabid Alabama football fans and have heard the frenzied, seemingly half-crazed crowd fall immediately silent when an opposing player was on the field injured. Comparing modern American football to barbaric gladiatorial culture is misguided at best and outright deceitful at worst.

Football has always had its critics (we will consider some of them in chapter 6), but don't allow such people to steal your enjoyment as a fan of the pageantry and excitement of the gridiron. Instead, thank God for the humanity of football.

Dirt, Dads, Diamonds, and the Church

I have a confession to make. When I attend a baseball game, I feel kind of like I do when I go to church. My children stay home from school on Major League Baseball's Opening Day because I have declared the day a cherished family holiday. I love baseball. It has been the background music of my life, and I have only turned up the volume with age. Among the ritual sounds of spring, there are none more significant to me than the popping of baseball glove leather and the bat connecting with the ball. Baseball is uniquely a game of particularities, people, and place. At any moment I can think back to my Brevard Avenue backyard pitching to my dad or relive the thrill of a Friday night game at tiny Joe Marshall field in Montgomery, Alabama.

I remember as a kid the first time my family headed east on I-85 from Montgomery to Atlanta to watch our beloved Atlanta Braves at old Fulton County Stadium. Today, I am glad that old, stadium-style facility was put out of its misery in favor of an actual ballpark. But as a boy, turning off of the concourse toward the field and seeing that perfectly manicured diamond for the first time was one of the most breathtaking sights I had ever laid eyes upon. The familial and cultural rootedness of baseball makes its fans nostalgic about the game and zealous for its history, heroes, and statistics. The game itself is timeless, not bound by a clock, but the past is always present in baseball.

I still consider a perfectly manicured ballpark one of the most beautiful works of art to be found in our world. The late baseball commissioner Bart Giamatti was fond of talking about the unusual symmetry and beauty of the game and its parks. When traveling, I always try to work in time to visit a ballpark or two—and no game need be played at the time. The simple enjoyment of taking in the confident uniqueness and beauty of a well-worn and well-kept ballpark is enough to savor.

I have always appreciated the fact that baseball fans are not simply drawn to the atmosphere of the event like many football fans are (for many, tailgating is the main event and the game is anticlimactic). Generally, baseball fans love the game and all of its quirky nuances. This love for the game never begins in the abstract. There is always a particular time, place, and person. Have you ever noticed when baseball players are asked about the origination of their love of the game, most often, their first words are, "my dad" and then at some point "there was this little park in my hometown . . ."? Catch with Dad, countless conversations, and the soil of a particular baseball diamond are most often the initial ingredients of devotion to the game.

When you arrive at the ballpark of your favorite team a couple of hours early (after all, infield and batting practice possess a beauty all their own), the other people you see are ethnically, socioeconomically, and culturally diverse, but most have essentially the same story: Dad, catch, and a Little League diamond in their hometown. A time, place, and person provides a wonderful rootedness in a transient rootless culture. It also explains why people who sit beside one another at baseball games almost always chat. They talk about the game they are watching and their general love of the game. No matter how different their backgrounds, they often possess a common metanarrative as it relates to their love of the great game.

However, as much as I appreciate the inherent beauty of an empty ballpark and its idiosyncratic design, it was built for a game to be played and the stands to be filled. No day in sports possesses the excitement and hopefulness for me of Opening Day. A baseball season does not simply begin; it is celebrated, from tiny, dusty, rural diamonds to Yankee Stadium. Unlike any other sport, the beginning of a new baseball season births a newness and hopefulness that this just may be the year for your favorite team. There is a sense, as Thomas Boswell has written, that time begins on Opening Day.

This hopefulness is warranted because baseball depends as much on the intangibles as it does 40-yard dash times and bench press maxes. A baseball equivalent of the NFL combine would be essentially worthless. You can't measure what made Pete Rose a great player, and baseball team success depends a great deal on clubhouse chemistry. It has always struck me how ordinary baseball players often look out of uniform. I remember as a teenager in Montgomery, Alabama, meeting Oscar Gamble (hometown baseball hero) and being amazed he hit two hundred big league home runs when he was no bigger than I was. As you drive to the park or turn on the TV to watch your favorite team on

Opening Day, you are right to be full of hope. This could be their year.

I also love the rhythm of baseball. One of the greatest features of baseball is the 162-game regular season. The uninitiated see the length of the season as a knock against baseball, but it is the very element that makes the game such a powerful metaphor for life. A sport where one loss ruins an entire season and perfection is an attainable goal is at odds with the managed failure of our actual lives. The 2011 World Series champion St. Louis Cardinals lost 72 games that season—that's 45 percent of the regular season. Miguel Cabrera led the Majors with a .338 batting average, which means his failure average was .662. He managed failure in the pursuit, not of perfection, but of greater consistency. Now that is something that resonates with my daily Christian life.

As much as I love and enjoy the game of baseball, it pales when compared to my love and enjoyment of the gathered church. One of my favorite moments every week is walking in to the worship center and seeing the eternally hope-filled faces of people from different ethnic, socioeconomic, and cultural backgrounds. Ordinary people involved in extraordinary work. The church assembled is a group of people who would never have gotten together if not for the fact that they possess a common metanarrative as it relates to the saving love of Jesus Christ.

Their stories are all different, and yet, at their core, they are all the same. They did not begin to follow Christ in the abstract. There was a time, place, and person when they heard the Good News of Jesus Christ and believed. Now their lives are forever rooted in his grace.

As they gather for a church service to celebrate the resurrected Christ, they have struggled all week and often failed, but their goal is not perfection (their Savior was a perfect substitute in their place) but simply greater consistency. The Lord's Day is a precious gift built into the rooted rhythm of our lives. Every Sunday is full of newness and hope through faith in Jesus Christ no matter our failure.

Baseball is not heaven, and it is not a glorious taste and window of heaven on Earth like the church. But I do confess, baseball reminds me of church, and for that I am glad. Louis R. Tarsitano, writing on the importance and similarities of the mystery of baseball and biblically faithful church worship, explains that people are drawn to seek mysteries seriously because they need "a time, a place, or a Liturgy" where they can encounter the overwhelming mystery. There are rooted temporal echoes of that ultimate mystery in places like baseball, but the incomparable embodied encounter with the mystery of the kingdom of God "requires a Church that will share and teach her mysteries, but not compromise them or apologize for them."[10] Missiologist Lesslie Newbigin wrote, "The geographical parish can never become irrelevant or marginal."[11] Newbigin is right, and we can also conclude that geographical cultural echoes of the church, like sports, will never cease to be valuable to God's image bearers.

We long for a place where we truly belong, where we are rooted, even as we eagerly await the ultimate consummation of Christ's kingdom in a new heaven and new earth. The more placeless society becomes, the greater the longing for a place to call home will become, even as we pray, "Your kingdom come, your will be done, on earth as it is in heaven" (Matt. 6:10). As Christian sports competitors and fans, we grow to reflect God by loving particular places and people. We share a narrative memory, a common story, that involves ultimate things, but that also involves temporary but treasured things that uniquely bind us to particular people at a particular time in history. Gnosticism is an ancient heresy that never fully vanishes away. It holds contempt for physical places and matter in favor of the spiritual and abstract. Gnosticism is not Christian. The gospel comes to Christians in particular localities and transforms place for God's glory (1 Cor. 10:31). Your enjoyment of sports and many other daily cultural realities can become a powerful, providential reminder of grace as G. K. Chesterton's poem explains:

> *You say grace before meals,*
>   *All right*
> *But I say grace before the play and the opera,*
> *And grace before the concert and the*
>   *pantomime,*
> *And grace before I open a book,*
> *And grace before sketching, painting,*
> *Swimming, fencing, boxing, walking, playing,*
>   *dancing;*
> *And grace before I dipped the pen in the ink.*[12]

Distinctively Christian Gospel Fanatics Who Enjoy Sports

If, as Chesterton asserts, we can say grace over our enjoyment of sports, then we must think about our enjoyment of sports in light of the priority of our faith and the supremacy of Jesus Christ. What would a distinctively Christian approach to sports look like? In the Sermon on the Mount (Matt. 5—7), Jesus teaches about the characteristics of the kingdom of Christ. His message turns the wisdom of the world upside down and is a call for his disciples to live distinctive lives. The distinctiveness of Christ's followers will bring verbal and even violent persecution at times (Matt. 5:11–12) because the disciples of Jesus constitute an alternative kingdom community who are in the world but not of the world (John 17:14–15). In other words, Christians are to constitute a unique gospel culture within a culture. Let us consider what Jesus' call for his followers to be salt and light means for how we think about our interaction with sports as Christians.

First, a distinctively Christian approach to sports must actively seek to preserve the good in God's cultural gift of sports. Jesus told a tiny band of Palestinian peasants with no cultural power or authority, "You are the salt of the earth" (Matt. 5:13). Before refrigeration, salt was used to preserve meat from inevitable decay and to season food. Animals are a part of the good creation of God and are used as food to nourish and sustain his image bearers. Meat, not preserved, will rot and be harmful, but meat properly preserved and seasoned can become, not just good, but very good. Jesus then provided two warnings. The first is that salt contaminated and diluted is worthless, and the second is that its saltiness, once lost, cannot be restored (Matt. 5:13).

The implication for Christians in relation to sports is clear. If Christians uncritically absorb sports culture, they will have no preserving influence. But, they will also be ineffective if they withdraw from sports culture.

Contaminated salt and unused salt are simply different pathways to decay. When Christians are absorbed into the culture or withdraw from the culture, they are forsaking their responsibility to be "the salt of the earth." The result of Christian unfaithfulness in this way is cultural decay and darkness. Christians who providentially grew up in areas and within families where a value and love for sports has been passed on to them must not engage in athletics as a participant or fan in a passive way but rather as those who have "decided to know nothing among you except Jesus Christ and him crucified" (1 Cor. 2:2).

Second, a distinctively Christian approach to sports will seek to illumine the world. I wonder if you have ever been in real darkness. Once touring a cave in Chattanooga, Tennessee, our guide turned off all the lights, and I could not see my hand though it was an inch from my face. It was an eerie and frightening experience. In a world marked by darkness, dimly lit by common grace and general revelation, Jesus tells this tiny band of followers, "You are the light of the world" (Matt. 5:14). I cannot imagine how outrageous that claim must have sounded.

Israel had been called to be "a light for the nations" (Isa. 42:6), and Jesus would claim to be on mission as "the light of the world" (John 8:12). And because his followers were to reflect him and the values of his kingdom, they are to be "the light of the world," described as "a city set on a hill," and "a lamp," not to be covered or hidden (Matt. 5:14–15). In other words, the preserving work of Christians as "the salt of the earth" and their illuminating work as "the light of the world" is to be a communal blessing—a public good. Therefore, the light of the Christian gospel should permeate all public places, including the athletic fields and stands.

The people of God have not been given the light of Jesus simply so that they can personally enjoy it. Neither have they been given the light so that they can share it with each other or compare to see whose lamp shines the brightest. Nor have they been given the light so that they can shake their heads and talk about those sad and pitiful people of the world who grope around in darkness. No, they are to be "the light of the world." The pervasive cultural interest in sports provides a particular, specific, and strategic place for Christians to be the light of the world.

Third, a distinctively Christian approach to sports will be God-centered and God-directed. In other words, it will be for the glory of God. Jesus says, in the same way a lamp shines, and a city on a hill cannot be hidden, Christians are to let their distinctive gospel light shine for the benefit of others, "so that they may see your good works and give glory to your Father who is in heaven" (Matt. 5:16). The Christian is not given distinctiveness in order to parade their virtue and righteousness before the world. Doing that is simply a manifestation of pride—not salt and light. When Christians do so, they are adding to the decay and darkness. The goal is not that others would see them and follow their morality but that they would glorify God in Christ.

Let Your Light Shine

Our salt-work of preserving the culture provides us points of contact with people who do not follow Jesus or live in the light of the gospel. Sports, music, art, drama,

cooking, building, creating, and countless other manifestations of culture are enjoyed by both Christians
and non-Christians. The Christian's light-work is to
point out how his or her appreciation and enjoyment of
cultural manifestations of truth, beauty, and goodness
point to the glory and grace of God. Culture always
begins with God as we can only be culture makers
because of his work as Creator. Jesus' call for us to be
the salt of the earth and the light of the world means
that we should not simply condemn sports culture
and withdraw from it and that we should not uncritically absorb sports culture. When we do either, we are
hastening cultural decay and darkness and forfeiting
Christian distinctiveness.

Rather, Christians should participate in a cruciform
engagement with and celebration of sports culture as
capable of reflecting the truth, beauty, and goodness
of God. When Christians live daily as the salt of the
earth and the light of the world, our Christian theology
intersects with our geography, and we are liberated in
our daily lives to do all—including sports—to the glory
of God. I'm thankful that I was taught as a child to say
"Roll Tide," but believe it or not, I'm equally thankful
that others say, "War Eagle." Yet, I am most thankful
that—whether we are Aggies or Longhorns, Cats or
Cardinals, Buckeyes or Wolverines, Ducks or Beavers—
in Christ we all say, "Come, Lord Jesus!" (Rev. 22:20).

Chapter Three

Sports and Spiritual Warfare

*Share in suffering as a good soldier of Christ
Jesus. No soldier gets entangled in civilian
pursuits, since his aim is to please the one who
enlisted him. An athlete is not crowned unless
he competes according to the rules. It is the
hard-working farmer who ought to have the first
share of the crops. Think over what I say, for the
Lord will give you understanding in everything.*

(2 Timothy 2:3–7)

Blitz, bomb, blown away, formation, trenches, neutral zone, red zone, offense, defense, attack, press, assault, battle, battle-plan, field general, no man's land, battle-tested, and so on. Anyone who listens to sporting figures, analysts, and commentators knows that the language of athletic competition and the language of military combat share a vocabulary. There is a sense in which all athletic competition is an artificially designed mock battle. Of course, there is a danger in the comingling of sports and warfare language. Actual warfare is horrific, and in comparison, sporting battle is merely trivial. Nonetheless, when kept in proper perspective, the shared language can be helpful for the Christian since the biblical story line is a story of spiritual war. Thus, it is not surprising that the Bible seizes both military warfare and sports competition as analogies for Christian living.

The Christian life *is* spiritual warfare. The biblical story begins with serpent-inspired conflict in the garden and ends with a glorious celebration of triumphant victory in a new heaven and a new earth: "There were loud voices in heaven, saying, 'The kingdom of the world has become the kingdom of our Lord and of his Christ, and he shall reign forever and ever'" (Rev. 11:15). When Christ returns he will consummate his kingdom and reign victorious over "that ancient serpent, who is the devil and Satan" (Rev. 20:2) and put a final end to his parasitic kingdom opposition. The church lives as the outpost of the kingdom of Christ in the time of the overlap of the ages, the already/but not yet of the kingdom. Therefore, the Christian lives in the context of a cosmic spiritual battle, though the warring kingdoms are not evenly matched and the outcome in Christ is secure (Eph. 6:12; Col. 1:13). We are called to fight against sin as good soldiers of Christ Jesus who proclaim the gospel no matter the cost (Eph. 6:12–17; Phil. 1:30; 2:25; Heb. 12:4; 1 Pet. 2:11; Jude 3; 2 Tim. 2:3–4; 4:7).

Onward Christian Soldier and Athlete

The New Testament language for sports competition is instructive and mirrors the language of warfare. The word *athlete* comes from the Greek word *athleo,* which means "to compete" (2 Tim. 2:5). Our word *agony* comes from the Greek word *agon,* which means "fight, struggle, or conflict" (Phil. 1:30; Col. 2:1; 1 Thess. 2:2; 1 Tim. 6:12; 2 Tim. 4:7; Heb. 12:1), and related to *agon* is the Greek word *agonizomai,* which means "to fight or strive against" (Luke 13:24; John 18:36; 1 Cor. 9:25; Col. 1:29; 4:12; 1 Tim. 4:10; 6:12; 2 Tim. 4:7). *Gymnasium* comes to us from the Greek word *gymnasia,* which means "exercise or training for competition" (1 Cor. 9:24–27; Gal. 2:2; 5:7; Phil. 1:30; 2:16). According to Paul, if athletes agonize to fulfill determined temporal goals, how much more should he and others agonize in gospel ministry? These qualities are why "Paul is fond of both military and athletic metaphors," as Ralph Earle notes.[1] Both the athlete and the soldier need single-minded focus and the incentive of victory. Each must endure hardship and agonizingly strive in preparation and disciplined training for conflict. *The Dictionary of Biblical Imagery* provides an excellent summary of the New Testament lessons Christians should glean from athletic competition:

> Athletic images conjure up a number of stimulating associations, including rigorous training or exercise (1 Cor. 9:25; 1 Tim. 4:7–8), singleness of purpose (1 Cor. 9:26), delayed gratification (1 Cor. 9:25), streamlining for maximum performance (Heb. 12:1), self-control (1 Cor. 9:27),

perseverance (Heb. 12:2) and endurance (1 Tim. 4:8). Athletic endeavor also involves intense competition with lofty objectives (1 Cor. 9:24) and high stakes (Eph. 6:12), and it requires faithful adherence to a prescribed set of rules to avoid disqualification (2 Tim. 2:5; 1 Cor. 9:27). In spite of all the hard work, the end result is transitory fame. But for the Christian the crown to be won is imperishable (1 Tim. 4:8; 1 Cor. 9:25).[2]

If you are a sports fan, I am confident that you are already very familiar with at least one biblical Greek word, even if you have never studied New Testament Greek. It is the Greek word *nike*, or as you are probably more familiar with seeing it written, NIKE. Nike is probably the most recognizable sports brand in the world. Phil Knight and Bill Bowerman chose the Greek word *nike* for the name of their athletic shoe company because it carries the idea of victory, conquering, and overcoming. Craig S. Keener explains the use of the various forms of *nike* in the biblical book of Revelation: "'Overcoming' (especially a military or athletic image of conquest or victory) here involves persevering in the face of conflict and hardship; this is all that the Lord requires to secure ultimate victory" (Rev. 2:7, 11, 17, 26; 3:5, 12, 21; 5:5; 6:2; 11:7, 11; 13:7).[3] The Scriptures make a clear and positive connection between sports, warfare, spiritual warfare, and the pursuit of victory. Competing is not sufficient; it is of utmost importance to desire to win the contest within the rules of engagement.

It should surprise no one that General Douglas MacArthur (1880–1964), a military leader who loved athletics, had the following statement carved on the stone passageway that leads to the gym at the U.S. Military Academy:

> *Upon the fields of friendly strife*
> *Are sown the seeds*
> *That, upon other fields, on the other days*
> *Will bear the fruits of victory.*[4]

General MacArthur went so far as to order the student body to participate in intramural athletics and urged congressmen to recommend gifted young athletes to West Point.[5]

Oliver Wendell Holmes (1841–1935), a combat veteran of the Civil War who later served on the United States Supreme Court from 1902–1932, told the Harvard graduating class in 1895, "In this snug, over-safe corner of the world, we may realize that our comfortable routine is no eternal necessity of things, but merely a little space of calm in the midst of the tempestuous untamed streaming of the world." Holmes urged Americans to "be ready for danger" because peace is always fragile and we must always be prepared to sacrifice and fight for it. He counted athletics as one vital way Americans can prepare to be ready. He also endorsed physically demanding and tough combat sports by asserting, "I rejoice at every dangerous sport which I see."[6]

One of American football's early champions and innovators was a Christian coach named Amos Alonzo Stagg (1862–1965). He had been a theology student at Yale training to become a pastor but struggled mightily with preaching and decided, "After much thought and prayer, I decided that my life can best be used for my Master's service" as a football coach. Stagg was convinced that he "would be going away from rather than into [Christ's] vineyard by being ordained."[7] According to Stagg, football reflected military warfare because it was "a game of war within the limitations of the rules and of sportsmanship."[8] Stagg wrote, "As I view it, no man is too good to be the athletic coach for youth."[9] The discipline, focus, courage, and characteristics it takes to be a competitive athlete or loyal soldier also pertain to Christian living, and believers who enjoy sports ought to have eyes to see.

Sports: Abstracted from Christ or Summed Up in Christ?

Sports are a good gift from God, but like all of his good gifts, sports are corrupted and broken in our fallen world. Anyone who thinks that sports automatically cultivate good character simply is not paying attention or purposefully ignoring reality. Sports as ultimate turns a good thing into an idol. Idols are almost always good gifts of God that are treated like God—as the ultimate source of satisfaction. An idol carved out of wood and worshipped corrupts God's gift of wood. The same is also true when God gifts one of his image bearers with exceptional athletic ability, only for the athlete to respond by getting his or her identity and sense of worth from athletic gifting and success. When this happens, God's gift is turned into an idol. Whenever Christ is not at the center of our lives and personal identity, an idol quickly fills the vacuum. Sports treated as the end for which we are created are corrupting and character-destroying.

When Satan tempts, he does not need you to deny Jesus openly to corrupt your character and mute your testimony. Displacing Christ from the center of your life and using him as a means to an end, rather than the end for which you are created, will work just as well for his hellish purposes. Christ is to be the Christian's identity, context, center, and end; so all other desires, including sporting desires, are subordinate to Christ. That Christ-exalting fact should be liberating and not confining because it means that nothing can steal our contentment, including sporting failure and losses. Anyone who says, "Christ is useful," is worshipping and serving self, not Christ. The person who is worshipping and serving Christ understands that every circumstance is simply a unique setting to declare Christ as all-sufficient, beautiful, and glorious.

But herein lies a pervasive problem. Far too often, it is not only Christians who consider sports a waste of time, who struggle to see a place for sports in their faith commitment, but those Christians who enjoy athletics often treat sports as a sort of guilty pleasure. In other words, they abstract sports from following Christ as a disciple or they simply attempt to use Jesus for athletic empowerment and success. The problem is that Jesus never promised us athletic success, and he certainly never signed up to be a subcontractor on our sports kingdom building project. Our responsibility is to "take every thought captive to obey" Jesus (2 Cor. 10:5)—including our thoughts about sports. No matter our present address, Christians are elect exiles—sojourners—whose citizenship is in heaven (Phil. 3:20; 1 Pet. 1:1; 2:11). Our background, nationality, family identity, and interests like sports are not ultimate, but they do serve as concrete markers of our experience of God's expansive grace as long as we see them through the lens of Jesus Christ and him crucified (1 Cor. 2:2).

I Can Fumble and Strike Out through Christ Who Strengthens Me

I have always been somewhat amused but also troubled every time an athlete quotes Philippians 4:13 right after he or she scores the game-winning touchdown, hits a game-winning home run, nails game-winning free throws, or kicks the game-winning goal: "I can do all things through him who strengthens me." Have you ever noticed that no one ever quotes that verse after the game when he or she gave up the game-winning touchdown, struck out to lose the game, missed free throws that would have won the game, or missed a wide-open goal kick that would have sealed his or her team's victory? This phenomenon among Christian athletes reveals the way too many Christians who play sports think about their Christian commitment in relationship to sporting competition. It seems that they think about Christ only in relation to their successes as defined by playing well and winning. Such an approach flows from a triumphalist and self-referential understanding of their Christian faith.

In Philippians, the apostle Paul is calling for Christian joy and passionate living in the midst of the most difficult trials and circumstances. When Paul writes the letter to the Philippians from a Roman prison (AD 60–62), he wants the believers in the church at Philippi to understand that Christ is his identity and the center of his life: "For to me to live is Christ, and to die is gain" (Phil. 1:21). He also wants them to know that the context of his life and his goal, the end for which he exists, is Christ:

> Indeed, I count everything as loss because of the surpassing worth of knowing Christ Jesus my Lord. For his sake I have suffered the loss of all things and count them as rubbish, in order that I may gain Christ. . . . But one thing I do: forgetting what lies behind and straining forward to what lies ahead, I press on toward the goal for the prize of the upward call of God in Christ Jesus. (Phil. 3:8, 13–14)

Paul exhorts, "Brothers, join in imitating me" (Phil. 3:17) so that you can "Rejoice in the Lord always" (Phil. 4:4). By way of application near the end of Paul's letter to the church at Philippi, he declares, "I have learned in whatever situation I am to be content. I know how to be brought low, and I know how to abound. In any and every circumstance, I have learned the secret of facing plenty and hunger, abundance and need. I can do all things through him who strengthens me" (Phil. 4:11–13).

In the next verse Paul writes, "Still, you did well by sharing with me in my hardship" (Phil. 4:14 HCSB). Elsewhere, the apostle Paul declares, "For the sake of Christ, then, I am content with weaknesses, insults, hardships, persecutions, and calamities. For when I am weak, then I am strong" (2 Cor. 12:10). Are you beginning to pick up on a theme? A proper understanding of, "I can do all things through him who strengthens me," would lead to quoting it in the midst of athletic failure more often than during athletic success. The issue is never whether or not you score the touchdown, but how you trust and glorify Christ when you score the touchdown and when you do not. In other words, the issue is one of spiritual warfare. The problem is that many Christians do not think about their engagement with sports in terms of spiritual warfare to the glory of God, but rather as God helping them to be more successful. But what if failure provides you a strategic and unique opportunity to glorify God?

Baseball provides many helpful lessons for those engaging in spiritual battle because it is a game that inherently means dealing with failure. "There is more Met than Yankee in all of us," as Roger Angell poignantly wrote in *The Summer Game*.[10] Every person who has ever played the game of baseball has been a consistent failure. It has been more than seventy years since the Splendid Splinter, Ted Williams, finished the 1941 baseball season with a .406 batting average. Williams's failure rate of 60 percent means that he failed less often than any batter in the seven subsequent decades. In fact, only five other players in the live ball era (since 1920) have matched the success of his 60 percent failure rate. Babe Ruth, known for hitting 714 home runs, struck out 1,330 times in his Major League Baseball career. The Cy Young Award is baseball's most coveted honor for the game's best pitcher each season, yet the award's namesake lost 316 games as a major league pitcher. Baseball requires a kind of moral courage that keeps persisting in the face of inevitable repeated personal failures. That is the sober, unalterable reality for Major League Baseball Star Mike Trout and every little leaguer as well.

Baseball does not fit well with the current trend of sports leagues that do not keep score and where the goal is for everyone to be successful and know that they are always a winner. Such a notion does violence to a game that is structurally committed to constant reminders of the participant's finitude and allows no room for such utopian fantasies. One of the reasons baseball was slow to embrace instant replay (2008, the last of the four Major North American Sports Leagues) in the sport is that a game marked by chronic managed failure propagates no delusions of human perfectionism in its players or its umpires. When a baseball purist asserts, "Bad calls are a part of the game," he is saying something about the warp and woof of the game.

Only genuine baseball fans understood the reaction of Detroit Tigers pitcher Armando Galarraga during the 2010 baseball season when he was one out from throwing a perfect game (it would have been the twenty-first in Major League Baseball history) and veteran umpire Jim Joyce made one of the worst big-moment calls in baseball history. Joyce, inexplicably, called the batter safe at first base. When the next batter was retired, Galarraga was saddled with the most disappointing one hitter in the history of the game. How did Galarraga respond to the injustice? When it happened he offered a stunned grin and after the game he said, "He is human. Nobody's perfect . . . I want to tell him not to worry about it." That moment was a beautiful window into what makes baseball unique.

Persistent, daily plodding in the face of chronic managed failure, driven by future hope, sounds a lot like my daily Christian walk. The apostle Paul wrote, "For I do not understand my own actions. For I do not do what I want, but I do the very thing I hate" (Rom. 7:15). But he went on to write, "Thanks be to God through Jesus Christ our Lord! . . . There is therefore now no condemnation for those who are in Christ Jesus" (Rom. 7:25; 8:1). The reality of his persistent failure and limitations did not paralyze him because he knew his story fit into a larger picture of the story of Christ. In the kingdom of Christ, "all things work together for good, for those who are called according to his purpose," and those who love God are being conformed to the image of Christ (Rom. 8:28–29).

Every 162-game baseball season—a seven-month exercise in hopeful, managed failure—is a faint echo of the glorious promise James offers to all who have put their faith in the Lord Jesus Christ: "Count it all joy, my brothers, when you meet trials of various kinds, for you know that the testing of your faith produces steadfastness" (James 1:2–3). Everyone has the tendency to compare the highlight reel of others' successes to our daily failures and lose heart. But baseball, for those of us who love it, provides a constant reminder that everyone (even the superstar) strikes out, but the game still goes on. Angell was right, "There is more Met than Yankee in all of us," and there is a glimmer of a greater glory that historically frequent losers like the Mets keep taking the field. But we must also realize that sometimes sports become an idolatrous weapon wielded against God.

When Sports Become Our God

For many of us, our cultural story and family story includes a love of sports and allegiance to certain sports teams. I don't have to sit around and wonder how I became an Alabama football fan or Atlanta Braves fan. I am both because my father cheered wholeheartedly for both. We went to games at Bryant-Denny Stadium and Fulton County Stadium. We wore Alabama shirts and Braves hats. My mother made special meals on big game days, and we celebrated the victories of the teams with which we identified. It is a part of my story, my place. As hard as it is for me to imagine, if I had been born in a different region, I might even appreciate soccer and other sports that hold little interest to me now.

However, there are those whose preoccupation with sports becomes all-consuming, turning a good thing into something ultimate—a competitive religion. Below are some guidelines to help you decide whether or not you are corrupting God's good gift of sports. Is your commitment to sports as a participant or fan becoming a substitute god rather than a means of delighting in God?

Do you enjoy sports as a good gift of God even when your team loses?

Finding idolatrous excesses in one's devotion to sports competition as a player or excessive devotion to a particular sports team as a fan is not difficult, tragically, even among professing Christians. In my home state, the Alabama-Auburn rivalry has been connected to incarceration, divorce, violence, and recently, the poisoning of majestic trees that were a part of one of the grandest traditions in college football. For such people, allegiance to a favorite team is not an enjoyment of God's good gift of athletics or a rooted cultural identity marker but an obvious idol. Most who read this chapter will never contemplate such atrocious acts; however, idolatry that is subtler is no less an act of rebellion.

If you cannot delight in God with thanksgiving for a hard-fought contest when your team loses, then you are perverting God's good gift of athletics and teaching those around him to do the same. Christian parent, if you cannot root like crazy with your children for your favorite team—only to see them lose—and afterward laugh and play in the yard with your kids, you have a problem; it's called idolatry. I have known children who desperately wanted their dad's favorite team to win, not because they cared all that much, but because they knew their father would be sour the rest of the day if they lost. Such behavior is pathetic for one whose identity is in Christ.

Do you sever your participation in sports or cheering for your favorite team from your Christian commitment?

I once knew a godly man who just happened to have season football tickets for the local college team and invited me along to attend a game. During the middle of the game, I was stunned when he blurted out an occasional profanity that I had never before heard him utter. I couldn't believe what I was hearing. His demeanor was also aggressive and rude to those around him. When I saw him later at church or at his job, he was back to the godly and faithful man I had always known. At the stadium, the outcome of the game was functionally his lord, which is a problem for one who confesses that Jesus alone is Lord.

If your behavior at a game would make it awkward for you to shift the conversation to your faith in Christ, you are making an idol of sports. I have known Christians who prefer to watch games alone because they did not want others to observe the way they act during the games. Moreover, when sports are used as an excuse to neglect God and Lord's Day congregational worship, they are not a tool in discipleship but rather a distraction from discipleship. Abraham Kuyper's dictum should shape our interest in sports, "Oh, no single piece of our mental world is to be hermetically sealed off from the rest, and there is not a square inch in the whole domain of our human existence over which Christ, who is Sovereign over all, does not cry: 'Mine!'"

Does your involvement in sports inspire you to faithfulness in your vocation and endeavors?

Paul seizes the metaphor of sports as a key image to explain Christian living because success in athletics demands purposeful self-sacrifice and requires self-discipline for a cause greater than the individual (1 Cor. 9:24–27; Phil. 3:13–14; Gal. 2:2; Eph. 6:12; 2 Tim. 2:4–7; Heb. 12:1–2). A Christian approach to sports as a participant or as a spectator involves being inspired to delight in the Creator through witnessing the honed physical gifts and agonizing determination of his image bearers who compete with excellence. Therefore, Christians should be challenged to offer similar purposeful discipline and sacrificial devotion in their vocations and endeavors.

How many Christians rigorously critique the job performance, dedication, and work ethic of the coach of their favorite team while simultaneously complaining about their jobs and excusing their own lack of work ethic and dedication? Such is a sad commentary on their lack of commitment to the priority of the kingdom of Christ in their daily lives. Where this kind of Christian hypocrisy is happening, the love of sports has become detached from the Christian life and transformed into a barrier rather than a bridge to glorifying Christ. Christian fans should watch and enjoy the beauty, effort, and focus that the sporting contest brings out in its participants, and should be challenged to agonize in similar fashion for the glory of Christ in their own vocations (Col. 3:17).

Gift or Idol?

When I teach at conferences and seminars about a proper Christian engagement with sports, I usually begin by asking some questions. First, I ask people to raise their hands if they have ever served in the military. Then, I ask the attendees to raise their hands if they have ever made a living as a farmer. Finally, I ask those in attendance to raise their hands if they have ever competed in athletics and consistently watch sports. Every time I have done this, only a few people raise their hands in response to the first two questions, but almost every single hand in the room goes up for those who have competed in athletics and have consistently watched sports.

In 2 Timothy 2:1–7, Paul lists soldier, athlete, and farmer as the three key metaphors for the Christian life (also 1 Cor. 9:6–7, 24–27). Then Paul commands, "Think over what I say, for the Lord will give you understanding in everything" (2 Tim. 2:7). Paul says it is not enough to read these things, but we must set our minds on them and ponder them. The outcome of proper meditation on these metaphors will provide practical, apologetic, and evangelistic fruit for Christ's followers.

It would seem imperative for us that since most contemporary Christians with whom we minister only have a personal point of contact with one of those metaphors, it would serve us well to have a biblically informed understanding of athletics and competition. Paul does not consider thinking through the relationship of sports to our Christian life a trivial matter. Rather, Paul counts it as an aspect of our spiritual battle.

The Christian church historically has struggled with its relationship to sports. This struggle is appropriate since we are called to "take every thought captive to obey Christ" (2 Cor. 10:5). Unthinking rejection or unthinking embrace of sports is a failure of Christian discipleship. I believe that the Christian with a rightly ordered, Christ-centered worldview is uniquely in a position to enjoy athletic competition as a good gift from God and his or her sports loyalties as a demonstration of providential rootedness in time, place, family, and community. Nevertheless, for one's view of sports to be rightly ordered, he or she must be aware of the danger of rendering it an idol rather than a gift. We can make an idol out of country, family, or allegiance to our favorite sports team. Nevertheless, the gospel does not obliterate these cultural realities. Rather, the gospel reinterprets all of them in light of the gospel story and our responsibility to seek first the kingdom of God (Matt. 6:33; 1 Cor. 2:2).

Chapter Four

Sports and Christian Discipleship

*Do you not know that in a race all the runners
run, but only one receives the prize? So run
that you may obtain it. Every athlete exercises
self-control in all things. They do it to receive
a perishable wreath, but we an imperishable.
So I do not run aimlessly; I do not box as one
beating the air. But I discipline my body and
keep it under control, lest after preaching
to others I myself should be disqualified.*

(1 Corinthians 9:24–27)

I believe that God made me for a purpose. But he also
made me fast, and when I run, I feel his pleasure."
That memorable line is from the 1981 British historical
drama *Chariots of Fire*. It is the response Eric Liddell
gives when he's confronted by his sister for neglecting
his responsibilities before God to focus on competitive

running in preparation for the 1924 Olympics. His words are powerful because he does not see his athletic pursuit as neglecting God but as a means of glorifying God. Liddell strove to keep God at the center of his athletic pursuits, so much so that he, being a strict Sabbatarian, refused to bow to international pressure to compete in the 100-meter race in the 1924 Olympics because it was on a Sunday.

You do not have to be a strict Sabbatarian to appreciate and learn from Liddell's example. I do not hold to Liddell's views on the Sabbath, believing instead that the Lord's Day (Sunday) should be set aside for corporate worship and gospel rest in celebration of the resurrection of Jesus Christ. In my understanding, the Sabbath principle is already fulfilled in Christ, who is our rest. Nevertheless, the Lord's Day is a gracious gift to remind us that our lives are "in him," and the day should be honored until he consummates his kingdom and ushers in eternal rest in the new heavens and earth. Regardless of one's particular views on the Christian Sabbath, Liddell's example is instructive for Christian parents as they think through all the complexities of leading their children through participation in youth sports.

Sports as a Metaphor for the Christian Life

Eric Liddell's sister considered all sports to be a waste of time. As we noted earlier, that notion is still around. It is not uncommon to hear a Christian say something like, "Sports are not necessary; so, why waste time on them—time that could be better spent advancing the gospel?" On the contrary, the Bible is far from silent on sports and athletic competition and periodically uses sports imagery (Gen. 30:8; 32:24; Ps. 19:3–6; 2 Sam. 2:14; Phil. 3:13–14; Gal. 2:2; Eph. 6:12; Heb. 12:1–4). In fact, the apostle Paul holds up the athlete as one of his three primary metaphors, along with the soldier and the farmer, for describing the Christian life (2 Tim. 2:4–7). He also compares the discipline and self-control required for faithfully following Christ to a runner training for and competing in a race (1 Cor. 9:24–27). If Paul had lived in our age, I think it is safe to assume he would have had ESPN. As believers in Christ, we should follow Paul's lead in seeing athletic competition as a good gift from God—a gift that has the potential of providing lessons that can help us mature in Christ when rightly applied.

Sports and the Supremacy of Christ

As Christian parents, our responsibility is to teach our children "the supremacy of Christ in all things" (Col. 1:18)—including sports. Paul made clear that a far more important goal exists than winning a perishable wreath on an athletic field (1 Cor. 9:25). In an effort to prioritize Christ, some Christians pull their children out of sports altogether. They simply do not want to face the decisions that inevitably will arise while navigating athletic involvement and a commitment to church and Christian service. One of the problems with this short-sighted approach is that the kids playing on these teams will one day grow up to have jobs, children of their own, and other responsibilities as they serve Jesus and his church. It is simplistic and unrealistic to teach our children that we can push "pause" on the rest of life to focus on Jesus. Showing them how to navigate these matters while faithfully committing to the supremacy of Christ is not a problem but a wonderful opportunity for discipleship. The tension of prioritizing Christ in the midst of a busy schedule is something they will face for the rest of their lives. Sports commitments provide Christian parents a unique context in which to model the same kind of Christ-exalting decision making we find in Eric Liddell.

Some Christians make the mistake of prioritizing sports over church by reasoning that the youth sports opportunity is only for a limited period of time and the church will always be there. Clearly, teaching children that sports provide a valid reason to neglect God is disastrous. Some parents even fashion themselves as victims in dealing with these issues as though they cannot set boundaries on their children's participation. They reason as if the only options are not participating in sports at all or acting like the team's practice and game schedule is in charge of their children's lives.

Sports Are Not the Problem

The solution is simpler than many Christian parents want to believe, but it involves parental leadership, direction, and conviction. The bottom line is that sports are never the problem; inadequate leadership in the home is the problem. Sports are often made scapegoats for a parental failure of leadership. Liddell's excellent Christian example is instructive. He was passionately committed to excellence in athletic competition, but it was for the glory of God. Because God's glory was his end goal, his Christian conviction led him to set boundaries and gladly endure the consequences. When a Christian family is involved in sports, they should be committed and diligent participants, but they should also draw whatever boundaries are needed regarding their child's participation. As the father of eight children who loves sporting competition, I have had to lead my family in this way many times.

When you register your children to compete on an athletic team, you should clarify any boundaries that you have regarding their participation. For instance, when my children have played youth sports, we have told the leagues when we sign up that we do not play or practice on Sundays. With that information in mind, a coach is free to decide whether or not he wants our children on his or her team. Also, when our sons made all-star baseball teams, we told the coaches that we know most of the championship games are on Sundays and that our boys would not be able to participate on Sundays. If they did not want our boys on their teams because of that, we would certainly understand. It is beneficial to teach your children that Christian convictions have consequences and that you will gladly face them. Too many parents are rearing their children in Christian sentimentality, which seeks to allow them to have convictions for which they never have to suffer. Christian sentimentality is at odds with the gospel of Jesus Christ.

In our home we do not treat other church activities the same way we treat the Lord's Day. We have biblical-theological convictions that demand setting aside Sundays, but we do not have the same approach to general church programming. We are not victims of the team's schedule or the church program schedule.

Parents have the primary responsibility to disciple their children, and a major part of that discipleship involves our children watching the choices we make. For instance, if one of my children has practice or a game during the time of a church youth event, then they usually go to their practice or game because we want to glorify God with the commitment we have made to the team. In other words, we do not want to use general church activities as an excuse to be lax in our other commitments. We also view participating on the team and being involved as parents in the league or school as unique mission opportunities of which we want to take full advantage.

I have found that, if you are honest and straightforward from the beginning about what you will and won't do based on your Christian convictions, most people will respect you more, not less. Sports, rightly understood, are just one means to the greater end of delighting in God. Sports must not become an idolatrous competitor with God instead of a means to glorify him.

I believe that God made me for a purpose and that he placed me in a home that enjoyed sports, and when I played sports (particularly baseball), I felt his pleasure. I unapologetically hope my children feel his pleasure through their participation in sports as well.

Sports Expose Character

Another practical issue that parents face in guiding and leading their children through the highs and lows of athletic competition is how to respond to a child's performance. How hard should we push our children toward athletic excellence in sports? How important should sporting success be? Is having fun all that really matters? We have all seen parents who seem to be pushing their kids in an unhealthy way. A 2014 article by Brad Griffin from the Fuller Youth Institute (research-based training for Christian youth workers and parents) rightly takes issue with this dynamic of parents obsessing over a child's on-the-field performance. He writes, "All kinds of parental anxiety and dysfunction plays out on the sidelines and in the bleachers, and you only need to walk to your local park to catch a glimpse for yourself."[1] In fact, if we look close enough, we might not even need to leave our home to see this type of dysfunction.

Griffin's article rightly diagnoses a genuine and prevalent problem in many families, but I find his solution inadequate. He suggests, based on psychological research, that parents limit their comments to their children who compete in sports to the six healthiest statements moms and dads can make. The statements are:

- Before the competition:
  - Have fun.
  - Play hard.
  - I love you.

- After the competition:
  - Did you have fun?
  - I am proud of you.
  - I love you.

While all of these statements are helpful, they are far from sufficient in utilizing a child's participation in sports as a tool for cultivating Christian discipleship and a cruciform worldview.

Surely Griffin would not provide the same advice to parents regarding a child's work in school. What if the child has fun in school because he or she enjoys being the class clown? What if the fun he or she has competing in sports is because he or she plays selfishly or does not execute what the coach tells him or her to do? Should a parent always be proud of a child after competition no matter his or her effort or lack thereof? It seems to me that Griffin's advice trades a self-centered parent's obsession about performance for a self-centered apathy about competition and the priority of team.

Christian parents must say far more than, "I love to watch you play," to their children. I suggest parents say, "I love to watch you compete because it gives us a window into your character that we can shape and form as we focus on Christ." After all, Paul's admonition, "So, whether you eat or drink, or whatever you do, do all to the glory of God" (1 Cor. 10:31), demands self-sacrificial focus and effort that cannot be promoted through sentiment alone. Playing sports "heartily, as for the Lord" (Col. 3:23), will often be visible in sweat, bruises, and occasionally blood.

Sports and Self-Denial

One of my favorite stories related to the cultivation of Christian character in youth sports comes from a friend of mine whose son is a fantastic baseball player. His son was playing first base for his team in a big tournament game and made an uncharacteristic error that cost his team the lead. His son's response was to drop his head and slump his shoulders in self-pity. When he was in the dugout during the rest of the game, he sat on the bench and pouted over his mistake.

My friend's son ended up coming to the plate in the final inning with the bases loaded and his team down three runs. With two outs and the game on the line, his son hit a grand slam walk-off homerun to win the game for his team. His coach awarded him the game ball for his performance, but his father was far more concerned with his son's character than his performance. He told his son that he would have to give the ball back to his coach and apologize to both his coach and his team-mates for his self-centered attitude during the game. The father told his son that he was not proud of his selfishness and that he hoped he would learn from this how to respond in a self-sacrificial and others-centered way that would honor Christ.

If the dad would have responded, "Did you have fun?" then his son would have certainly said, "Yes!" He would have then learned that his "fun" was contingent upon playing for his own satisfaction. If the dad would have said, "I am proud of you," then his response would encourage a self-centered performance-based attitude. Instead of responding in these unhelpful ways, my friend proved that he loved his son enough to use sports to teach him about something much more important than the game. My friend also proved that he loved to watch his son play so that he could learn the priority of self-sacrificial, others-centered effort.

Below are some gospel-centered options that I would recommend for parents to say to their children before and after competitions:

- Before the competition:
  - Enjoy the opportunity to compete.
  - Play in a self-sacrificial way that places your teammates and coaches ahead of yourself.
  - When you make a mistake, respond by cheering all the harder for your teammates.
  - When your teammates make a mistake, encourage them.
  - Honor the officials/umpires by showing respect and thanking them after the game.
  - Cheer as hard on the bench as you would if you were in the game.
  - I love you.

- After the competition:
  - What did you learn about yourself?
  - Did you compete to the absolute best of your ability with no regrets about your effort?
  - In what ways did you sacrifice for your team?
  - How did you respond when you failed?
  - Were you others-centered?
  - Did you honor your coaches and the officials/umpires? Did you thank them?
  - I love you.
  - I love to watch you play and to see you learn, through competing, about living for Christ.

The Glory of Bench-Warming

Something great happened a few years ago during basketball season for one of my sons. He sat the bench. You may be thinking that such news sounds more like a cause for depression than celebration—and at the beginning of the season, my middle-school son would have agreed with you. The truth is, I do not want him to want to sit the bench. I want him to try with every ounce of his ability to earn a starting position. Yet, I also want him to know how to be a leader even when he finds himself sitting on the bench despite his best efforts. In most sports leagues he participated in prior to middle school, the focus had been teaching the fundamentals of the game and giving everyone an opportunity to play. This philosophy, coupled with the fact that my son was consistently one of the better players on past teams, meant that he rarely spent much time on the bench. But in sports, as with other areas of life, greater age brings greater responsibility and accountability—not to mention a strong dose of maturing reality. On athletic teams this shift means, appropriately, a transition from playing time being given to playing time being earned. It also means recognizing that God has gifted some people with superior athletic ability.

My son was excited when team tryouts were announced. He made the team, practices began, and the team moved toward the start of the season. We decided he would get up before school in the morning and run two miles on the treadmill to increase his stamina. Yet, when the team began playing games, he rarely got off the bench, and I began to notice that his demeanor changed. He seemed disinterested and chatty. He was only engaged and focused when he was in the game. On the floor, he was loud and fiery. When he was on the bench, which was most of the time, he rarely left his seat, and his posture was relaxed and slouching.

I heard one parent say about his son in a similar situation, "Well, what do you expect when he is sitting the bench? You have to feel sorry for him working so hard and not getting to play." I do not understand that mentality. I was pleased that my son was on the bench. It provided an opportunity for us as his parents to teach him what God expects from him when he finds himself on the bench. It is actually the same thing required of him when he is a starter: that he would be a leader who uses every ounce of his ability and effort to glorify Jesus. I did not feel one bit sorry for him working so hard and not getting to play. The truth is, my son needed to be a role player on that team; and the truth is, most of us end up being role players in life, not stars or starters.

One day after a game I asked my son, "Why aren't you being a leader on your team?" He glanced up at me with a perplexed expression that seemed to indicate his bewilderment at whether I had seen him sitting the bench. From that point my son and I developed a strategy for leading from the bench. We sought to answer some questions. How can you sit on the bench in a way that says, "I am as committed to the success of the team here as I would be if I were shooting free throws with the game on the line"? How can you sit the bench and positively affect the other players on the bench and in the game? How can you sit the bench in a way that honors your coach?

Developing our plan began with honest evaluation. I told him, "On this team you are not among the most talented and do not deserve to play very much right now. And that is okay; you can figure out your role and do everything you can to help the team be the best it can be—which is what each player should do anyway." I was pleased to see that my son responded well to this honest call to courage and self-sacrifice. The truth is that the team as a whole is more important than any one player and that my son should fulfill his role for the good of the team. Even if his role was not glamorous, his response was a triumph over the selfish individualism that had reared its ugly head earlier in the season; he was learning about far more than basketball at that point. My son was learning a lesson about human pride, grace, temptation, and the wiles of the Evil One (James 4:6–7).

Below I've outlined the game plan that my son and I created. Perhaps someday you will have a son or a daughter who sits the bench—or perhaps that situation is already happening. If so, great! Seize the opportunity for the glory of Christ.

- Make sure your posture communicates that you are engaged. Sit on the edge of your seat.
- Be the loudest player on the bench cheering for your team.
- Leap from your seat every time your team scores or gets a turnover.
- Get out of your seat during time-outs; go out on the court and greet the players who are in the game.
- Talk only about the game to your teammates on the bench.
- Listen to everything your coach says when he speaks, looking him in the eye.
- Be the first one to volunteer if your coach needs something done.
- When you do get into the game, remember that you may not be the most talented player out

there, but you can be the toughest player; dive
for every loose ball, play tough, and never get
out-hustled.

- Make the more talented players better by being
  tough on them in practice; challenge them, and
  make them fight for everything they get.

Baseball, Dads, and Discipleship

Diana Schaub writes, "Without fathers, there is no
baseball, only football and basketball."[2] It was one of
those lines that paralyzed me when I read it. As a former high school coach, I began reflecting on just how
true that sentence was in my experience. In football it
was common for a young man with superior brawn or
athletic ability to begin playing the game successfully
at an older age with no background or former tutelage
in the sport. Height alone can equate to some measure
of basketball success at younger ages, and skills can be
honed in isolation with nothing more than a ball and a
hoop. I love football and basketball, but neither of those
avenues are true with baseball. In most cases, the way
a love of baseball is transmitted is through dads.

No boy will love and pass down the game of baseball simply because someone bought him a glove, ball,
and bat. He cannot play catch with himself, hit himself ground balls, or throw himself batting practice.
Much less will he ever figure out on his own what in
the world a squeeze, sacrifice, infield fly rule, frozen
rope, Texas leaguer, or balk means. The mechanics,
mystery, nuance, and jargon of baseball demand that
one be personally discipled in its craft and patiently

taught its excellencies. A baseball score book resembles mysterious hieroglyphics until the signs and symbols are enduringly given meaning by a learned tutor. Very little in baseball is seeker-friendly or self-evident, and few people pick up the game on their own.

Baseball is uniquely a sport that fathers pass on to their children. When Willie Mays speaks of his dad teaching him how to walk when he was six months old by enticing him with a rolling baseball, he is telling the story of baseball. Atlanta Braves first-baseman, Freddie Freeman, tells how his CPA father took a late lunch every single day so that he could throw him batting practice after school. After sixteen years in the big leagues, Chipper Jones headed home and had his mom video record his swing so his dad could help him rebuild it. In historian Doris Kearns Goodwin's memoir, *Wait Till Next Year,* she explains the formative role her father's love of baseball had on her life and career pursuits, "By the time I had mastered the art of scorekeeping, a lasting bond had been forged among my father, baseball, and me. . . . These nightly recountings of the Dodgers' progress provided my first lessons in the narrative art."[3]

It is not uncommon for friends to ask me how I can continue to love the game in light of exorbitant salaries and the shame of the steroids era. The answer is simple: my passion and love for the game did not begin in multimillion dollar parks with forty thousand seats, and it cannot be taken away by what happens there. It began with my dad rolling a baseball to me at six months of age and grew with countless times of catch, ground balls, and batting practice with my father.

The soil of little Joe Marshall Field in Montgomery, Alabama, will always be more sacred to me than Fenway or any other big league park. As we picked up balls after another round of hitting, those conversations between father and son helped usher me from boyhood to manhood. My dad taught me important lessons like how the DH (designated hitter) was a corruption of the game of baseball and many things far more important. I cannot separate those lessons from the game that provided a glorious context in which to learn them, nor would I want to. There is nothing Major League scandals can do to take that away from me. Similar testimonies could be shared by almost every true baseball fan.

I fear that the diminishing popularity of baseball in recent years has less to do with the sport and more to do with the diminishing popularity of intentional fatherhood in our culture. Absentee fathers have contributed to the cultural decline of baseball as the national pastime in America, but it must be noted that there are varying kinds of absentee fathers. Some tragically do not live in the home with their children, but others who are in the home hire or farm out much of the parenting. Even in Christian families, providing entertainment and paying for opportunities is often counted as engaged parental involvement because we have lost a theology of personal presence. The central reality of our Christian faith is the awe-inspiring truth that "the Word became flesh and dwelt among us" (John 1:14). In John 20:21, Jesus, the eternal Word who became flesh and dwelt among us, says, "As the Father has sent me, even so I am sending you." Ours is a technologically driven, cyber-saturated, smartphone age, where it is easy to confuse impersonal communication of information with the genuine communion of embodied presence.

The emergence of baseball academies, specialized paid instructors, and travel baseball teams is a symptom of a larger cultural problem. All of these opportunities can be helpful and have a place as a supplement to a player's baseball development, but they too often become substitutes for what has made the game of baseball great and deeply entrenched in American culture. Absentee dads, whether physically absent or emotionally absent, will not hand down a love and passion for baseball. A father who lacks the kind of patience to teach a game like baseball will probably not take time for other complex and mysterious things either—far more important things.

Every time I see a father fiddling with his iPhone while paying another man $40 an hour to sit a ball on a tee or soft toss for his son, I realize we are losing the game. Baseball is a game enamored with history and conversation, which have linked generations with a connectedness and shared language. The familial rootedness of baseball contributed to its emergence as the national pastime, and the hectic, virtual world we inhabit today makes its value largely unintelligible. Our industrialized, mass production culture has led to an unthinking value of quick, cheap, and disposable over slow, valuable, and lasting. The downgrade is evident in a full range of the performing arts—including sports.

It is not just baseball that demands a parent's engaged presence. The good news of Jesus Christ is a simple, yet infinitely profound message. The Bible takes us through the most important story in the history of the cosmos. The biblical gospel story has all kinds of twists and turns, nuances, and mystery (Eph. 3:3–10; 5:32; Col. 1:26–27). It is the story that defines every one of our personal stories. Passing on "the faith that was once for all delivered to the saints" (Jude 3) to the next generation takes time, patience, never-ending conversations (Deut. 6:4–9; Ps. 78:1–8), and presence.

Just like the dad dropping off his son with the baseball professionals, too many Christian parents act as if they do not have time to disciple their children in the gospel story. It is much easier and more efficient to drop them off and allow the "professionals" at the church with seminary degrees to take care of the serious religious stuff. Too many parents think that paying for their children to have the best opportunities and college choices is what really matters. They tend to prefer the gospel-tract approach to teaching faith and life: just the facts, hopefully they get saved, and make sure they get a good education and well-paying job. In a faith with a Savior who took on human flesh and dwelt among us (John 1:14), we ought to know better than to think such a faith can be transmitted so inattentively. Faithfully teaching our children about the glory of the incarnate, crucified, and resurrected Christ demands time, patience, and presence.

Without fathers, there is no baseball—and unfortunately, that is one of the smallest tragedies of absentee dads. There is a reason grown men have often cried when *Field of Dreams* ends with Ray playing catch with his dad. I fear we are heading toward a time when many men will be unmoved and puzzled by what they see as a strange ending to the movie. If so, we will have lost far more than baseball.

On Your Mark

Parents are responsible before God for leading their children to keep Christ at the center of athletic competition. Whether we are protecting the Lord's Day to prioritize worship with the local church, having conversations with our children to help them think rightly before and after competitions, or guiding them through the disappointment of bench-warming, Christian parents must lead with intentionality in every area of our children's involvement in sports. Every decision we make regarding sports communicates to our children what we value as ultimate. Let us lead in such a way that there is no question we value the glory of Christ above all else, and let us lead the way Christ did: remaining personally present and available for our children. May we hear, "Play ball!", the opening whistle, "On your mark," and countless other sounds of the sports we love as a call to discipleship.

Chapter Five

Sports and Self-Esteem

Then Jesus told his disciples, "If anyone
would come after me, let him deny himself
and take up his cross and follow me."

(Matthew 16:24)

In 2013, the Youth Association Football program in Keller, Texas, made national headlines because of a decision that many onlookers found scandalous.[1] What brought media from major metropolitan cities and national news organizations to investigate the actions of a youth football program in a small Texas town? They had the unmitigated audacity, in the eyes of many, to stop giving out participation trophies. According to the league's vice president, the action was to fight the pervasive and unhealthy sense of entitlement with which children grow up today. Leave it to independently minded Texans to stand up and defy the spirit of the age. However, I am troubled that a youth football program in Texas had to lead the way by voicing what biblically minded Christians should have been saying all along.

The apostle Paul could not think about the spiritual battle of Christian living without pointing to the obvious parallels drawn from his interest in athletic competition. Throughout these allusions, it does not seem to occur to Paul that one would ever compete in an athletic contest without trying to win: "Do you not know that in a race all the runners run, but only one receives the prize? So run that you may obtain it" (1 Cor. 9:24). In fact, he has no desire to "run aimlessly" (1 Cor. 9:26). For Paul, sports involve agony, strife, discipline, self-control, hard work, focus, intensity, and a desire for victory—just like the Christian life.

Paul makes it clear that the eternal reward of an incorruptible crown is far more important than winning a corruptible crown on an athletic field, but his point only makes sense in light of the appropriate desire to win on the athletic field (1 Cor. 9:25). A child who does not care if he or she wins in a sporting contest and one who cannot lose without throwing a fit both have troubling character problems that ought to be addressed by Christian parents. Self-centered rage is not a spiritual virtue, but neither is weak-willed apathy. Christian parents must defy the spirit of the age by teaching children cruciform ambition: "And whatever you do, in word or deed, do everything in the name of the Lord Jesus" (Col. 3:17).

When Everybody Is a Winner, Nobody Wins

Though not keeping score and handing out participation trophies in youth sports is often passed off as a Christian idea, the root of this kind of thinking is found in modern psychological theory and not in the Bible. In 1969, Nathaniel Branden published an article entitled "The Psychology of Self-Esteem." He argued that feelings of self-esteem were the key to success in life, and his notion became a foundational presupposition in education and child rearing for a generation of Americans. When this theory is applied to children, praise is detached from any actual achievement. In the *New York Times* best-selling book *NurtureShock: New Thinking About Children,* Po Bronson and Ashley Merryman conclude that the result of this thinking is a generation of American young adults who feel better about themselves though they achieve less and fear challenges.

Another recent study on the origins of narcissism in children concluded, "Narcissism in children is cultivated by parental overvaluation: parents believing their child to be more special and more entitled than others." The abstract of the study further explains, "Children seem to acquire narcissism, in part, by internalizing parents' inflated views of them."[2] Unfortunately, the "you are so special, so smart, so beautiful, so talented, so gifted—you can do anything you want to do and be anything you want to be" mantra is often internalized, and our children suffer because of it.

If feelings of self-esteem are the key to success in life, the thinking goes, then every child must be told he or she is a winner, and handed a trophy, even when he or she loses. A few years ago my oldest son's middle school football team lost a game by about forty points. When they announced the score after the game, stating who had won and who had lost, a mother of a player on our team leaned over the rail and yelled, "Don't listen to that! You didn't lose! You are all winners! You are winners!" This lack of awareness to the reality of the beatdown that we had all just witnessed provoked me to respond, "Not tonight. Tonight they're big losers." Everybody is not a winner, and Christian parents ought to be willing to fight for our children's right to lose.

Grave implications exist for nurturing children in this type of self-oriented flattery culture where no one ever loses and everyone gets a trophy. The Bible relentlessly kicks the legs out from under our misplaced self-esteem and calls us to humble Christ-esteem. There's a danger in telling children in sports (and other activities as well), "All that matters is that you participate, play nice, have fun, and feel good about yourself." The danger is that they might believe it. Sports do not build character; they dramatically expose character and provide Christian parents and coaches with a valuable opportunity to develop Christian character. Our culture says, "Believe in yourself," and Jesus says, "Deny yourself and follow me" (Luke 9:23). No one can do both.

Nice children who just want to have fun and who have been consistently rewarded for intentional underachievement with a trophy are being cultivated in a worldview that is antithetical to self-sacrificial Christian discipleship. An entitlement mentality is at odds with the gospel message and God's promise that it is "through many tribulations we must enter the kingdom of God" (Acts 14:22). If sports participation simply becomes another vehicle to prop up the notion that our children's desires and feelings are more important than the good of others (the team), we must not act surprised when they someday conclude that their desires and feelings are more important than the good of their family, church, and everything else, too. Narcissism, laziness, and self-protection are not fruits of the Spirit.

When parents and coaches turn off the scoreboards and hand out participation trophies as though celebrating winners and their achievements is unspiritual, sports are stripped of the essence that makes them such a valuable metaphor for the Christian life. The desire to win and receive the prize in athletic competition is the very thing Paul latches onto as a transferable concept for cultivating a single-minded focus on the advance of the gospel (1 Cor. 9:24–27). There are eternal winners and losers (Rev. 3:21), and we are to count the cost, take up our cross, and follow him because we know what is at stake. Our task demands courageous, self-sacrificial, Great Commission gospel warriors. At its best, athletics provide Christian parents and coaches a limited but genuine theater for the examination and cultivation of Christ-honoring characteristics.

When everybody is a winner, nobody wins. When everybody gets a participation trophy, everybody loses. Christian parents and coaches ought to know that better than anyone.

A Distinctly Christian Alternative

Above all people, Christian parents who understand the gospel of Christ should know that a smiley faced sentimental approach to child rearing is an impotent placebo for preparing their children for the spiritual war that is life. Over-praising children detached from achievement on the athletic field (and everywhere else) encourages them to live based on an image and makes them fearful they might be exposed as not being so special, smart, talented, beautiful, and gifted. Such parenting makes children inordinately self-conscious, fearful, and frequently discontent.

For instance, when a child misses free throws that could have won the basketball game, many parents respond by telling their child, "Don't worry about it, you will make the free throws next time." This is merely empty flattery and sentimentality that will produce fearfulness in the child, not courage or genuine confidence. Such a response produces false expectations, which lead to anxiety. How does the parent know the child will make the free throws next time? If they do not make the free throws next time, it will seem as if the child is letting the parent down based on the parent's expectations. A better approach would be, "It was a great game. That is why sports are so exciting. Let's keep working on your free throws. We can start shooting thirty free throws a night before bed and charting how many you make each day. When you get the opportunity again, let's work to try to be as prepared as we can."

Above all other priorities, a Christian parent's job is to create categories in the daily lives of their children that help make the gospel intelligible as they prepare them for adulthood, and this nonnegotiable duty certainly includes sports. Foundational to a Christian worldview is the truth, "God opposes the proud but gives grace to the humble" (James 4:6; 1 Pet. 5:5). Parents must exert authority over their children, not for their own sake as parents, but for their child's ultimate good and well-being. Teaching your children to live under appropriate authority is a gift that leads to contentment. A gospel-centered approach to parenting that cultivates a biblical worldview will not abandon honest conversation about the child's strengths *and* weaknesses. Athletic competition exposes character in a way that a diligent Christian parent or coach can seize upon to instruct the athlete to help develop his or her character and a gospel-centered worldview.

Your children are created in the image of God with a responsibility to honor and obey God, appropriate authorities, and you. Christian parents must love God and their children enough to demand obedience and honor from their children (Exod. 20:12; Eph. 6:1–3). Below are some suggestions on how sports can help Christian parents raise non-narcissistic children who have been taught the value of humility, submission, and hard work. I do not offer these suggestions as though they carry "thus-sayeth-the-Lord" authority, but as sanctified Christian common sense.

Tell your children the truth

No, really; tell them the truth. Do not tell them the empty delusional clichés like, "If you believe it, you can achieve it." If they are not very good at something say, "You are not very good at _____, so here is how you can work hard to get better, and if you do not get better, here is how you can still serve others or help your team." After all, very few people are *the* best at anything, but they can strive to be *their* best at whatever they do and value their contribution as a role player. This approach sounds a lot like Paul's description of life in the church (1 Cor. 12). Very few athletes are exceptional, but that fact does not diminish the value of athletic competition. Honest assessment of skills and directing focus on how they can bring value to the team in a limited but vital role is excellent preparation for every aspect of life.

Teach them how to respond to the word "no"

Saying "no" is a gift because maturity cannot take place without it. Parents who rarely say "no" to their children, or who only do so apologetically, are cultivating an entitlement mentality and setting them up for failure as adults. Winston Churchill famously and insightfully said, "Success is the ability to go from one failure to another with no loss of enthusiasm." Humbly hearing "no" from someone in authority and resourcefully pressing ahead with eagerness is a foundational life skill. Such ought to be obvious to a people who say, "Jesus is Lord." Sports are one of the few places left in contemporary society, outside of the military, where "no" is a common word and authority is exercised in the pursuit of a goal bigger than the individual.

Anthony Esolen, professor of English at Providence College and Christian writer, suggests in "What Sports Illustrate" that the church can learn a lot from the authority and demands of football:

> It punishes failure, sometimes cruelly. It demands a recognition of and obedience to authority; yet it understands that hierarchy, too, must submit to the common good. Its physical demands are unimaginable to those who have not experienced them; according to those who have known both, it makes boot camp look like a beauty pageant. Men who participate are under constant physical stress and are usually in pain. The enterprise

is dangerous. Though the institution has its glamor, most of the participants are relatively unknown, and most of them will also, quite willingly, participate by adopting roles that ensure their anonymity among all but the knowledgeable few. The institution requires giving oneself up, day after day.

He adds:

Will the young men listen to a word you are saying *when you are telling them they are wrong*? Will they obey *when you require from them sacrifice that their friends would consider absurd*? No one can do that, you retort? Football coaches do that for a living. Can you be, not den mother to emotional dependents, not archsongster of a liturgical club, but a master, a colonel, a vice-regent, a father who can eschew the moment of truce because he sees, for the hosts he loves and leads, a distant glory?

Can you give men the courage to suffer and obey and restore their lives to order, as did the stern, soft-spoken, Christian coach of the Dallas Cowboys, Tom Landry? Can you be the *head,* as Christ is the Head of the Church? Is that the aspiration you believe the Lord has placed in your heart?[3]

Sports, rightly understood, work in the opposite direction of an entitlement mentality. The person who answers to an authority outside of him or her, who is willing to say "no" to any individual for the greater good of the team, is learning something vital about the necessity of self-sacrifice and courage. The combination in sports of accountability, competition, instruction, and authoritative leadership stirs the passions and, when rightly directed, can help produce self-forgetful enthusiasm.

Always support the coach's decisions about playing time and strategy (even if they are wrong)

It is possible that your child is correct and that he or she is better than the kid who is starting in front of him or her on the team. But, who cares? The real issue is how the child responds to that situation. What good will come from you telling your child that he or she should be playing more and talking to the coach about more playing time? Instead, tell your children this: "Most coaches want to win, and if they thought you gave them the best opportunity to win, they would be playing you. If you want to play, then work harder and make it clear to the coach that you are the best option, but do not sit around and whine about it." What a great opportunity to learn to be an adult employee to the glory of God. No one is fit to lead until he or she learns how to submit to authority and commit to a goal that is bigger than his or her preferences.

Teach your children that it is not the job of the coach to adjust to them; it is their job to adjust to the coach. The coach is the authority on the team and not your child. Teach your child to assume that his or her coach knows more and is in a better position to make decisions in the best interests of the team. Also, the coach's role is to make those decisions and not the players or parents. That means that unless the coach does something immoral or unethical (and you need to have those discussions with your children as well), his or her authority should be honored on the team. The coach may very well make arbitrary decisions on the team and may even unfairly assign playing time or responsibilities. I call that great life preparation. Children who grow up policing fairness in others instead of focusing on their own effort are generally unproductive in the culture and in the church.

Demand your children use honorific titles

Using honorific titles cultivates a basic respect for authority and a willingness to recognize hierarchal structures and roles that God has wisely ordained. Demanding your children use Sir, Ma'am, Mr., Mrs., Doctor, Coach, Officer, President, Governor, and so forth, provides a daily theology lesson. It is detrimental to shaping a biblical worldview for a child to walk up to an older man and say, "Hey, Bob." Parents, do we really want to teach our children that they do not have to show respect for those in authority, regardless of whether they agree with the decisions of the authority figure? What happens when they disagree with you? Thus, you should never allow your child to call the coach of the team by anything other than "Coach" and his or her last name, and the officials of the game should be accorded the same respect because of their position. This policy should be enforced even if a sibling or relative is in the role of coach or official.

Male and Female, the Image of God, and Sports

We have all heard the cliché, "You can be anything you want to be." In fact, it has become such a dominant

mantra in culture that its validity is hardly ever ques-
tioned. But is it helpful? More important, is it true?

In 2014, the Little League World Series produced a
star player who transcended the sport, Mo'ne Davis, a
pitcher for the Taney Dragons from Philadelphia. The
4-foot-11-inch, 84-pound, Mo'ne was thirteen years old
and threw a fastball with the equivalent velocity of 90
mph in the Major Leagues. Mo'ne was also a girl, which
made the sensational story all the more compelling. She
was only the fourth American girl to play in the LLWS,
and she said baseball was not even her favorite sport—
basketball was. The reported crowd for one of the
games she pitched at the LLWS was 34,128. Her performance was so captivating that she was featured on the
cover of the iconic sports magazine *Sports Illustrated*.
On top of it all, she was poised and irresistibly charm-
ing in the face of all the attention.

Knowing my love of all things baseball, I was asked
at the time what I thought about Mo'ne Davis playing in
the LLWS against boys. My immediate response was,
"It's great. She has been amazing." I also felt compelled
to add, "But I would not allow my daughters that age to
compete in sports against boys."

I certainly do not think a case can be made that
it is inherently wrong or sinful for a thirteen-year-
old girl to compete against boys in baseball, and I am
definitively not attempting to make that case here. Of
course, if it were a combat sport like wrestling, boxing,
or football, that would be an entirely different matter.
As a Christian father in a world of gender confusion
and chaos, however, my wife and I think it would be at
odds with what we desire to cultivate in our sons (we
have three) and daughters (we have five) to have them

formally compete against the opposite gender beyond childhood.

We believe that all people, male and female, are created in the image of God. Men and women are divinely designed and gendered image bearers. Our gendered humanity images God in the world (Gen. 1:27). Our sexual distinctiveness reveals to us something important about God's nature. In our attempt to teach our sons and daughters a healthy biblical sexuality, we want to celebrate and champion God's design in their distinctive masculinity and femininity. We desire for them to think about male and female relationships as complimentary and not competitive. We do not want our daughters thinking in terms of being able to do anything a boy can do, and we want our boys to think in terms of fighting for girls and not competing against them (1 Cor. 11:8–10; 1 Pet. 3:7).

Masculinity and femininity are to be surrendered to God for his glory and not measured in competition with one another. The wonderful contrast and compliment of male and female in the world teaches us about God and should evoke our worship of God. The desire in our family is to delight in and nurture the uniqueness of God's design in a culture that seeks to minimize it.

Downplaying or ignoring the God-designed differences in male and female liberates no one. Telling a woman to measure her worth by how well she can compete against men in sporting competition, and other ways too, is demeaning to her femininity. So, while boys and girls can both learn a lot from sports, my wife and I think it's best for our sons and daughters to compete against their own gender (especially beyond childhood). Sports are simply one tool we attempt to utilize toward the goal of cultivating our sons and daughters into Christ-exalting men and women.

G. K. Chesterton wrote a short poem entitled "Comparisons" that reveals the folly of those who would claim that acknowledging gender differences necessarily means inequality.

> *If I set the sun beside the moon,*
> *And if I set the land beside the sea,*
> *And if I set the town beside the country,*
> *And if I set the man beside the woman,*
> *I suppose some fool would talk about one being*
>   *better.*

I hope we will remember Mo'ne as a courageous and poised young woman who had an amazing Little League World Series. Her effort, humility, and poise was an inspiration to many (including me), and she possessed many traits I hope my sons and daughters will emulate. But I thought it was tragic that her on-field success as a thirteen-year-old pitcher immediately birthed a cultural narrative asking whether or not she would become the first female to play Major League Baseball. Heaping those sorts of expectations on her creates a mentality that suggests her present accomplishments will be somehow validated only if she goes on to play high school, college, or professional baseball against men. Mo'ne was described in the *New York Times* as "A Woman Among Boys" at the Little League World Series.[4] I wish we had let her be a remarkable thirteen-year-old young woman who dominated the competition at that time and had a bright future ahead.

Lose Like a Champion Today

There is a myth that only the best players and superior athletes benefit from participating in sports. In my experience, the exact opposite is true. Often, the naturally gifted athlete does not benefit from athletics as much as the person who is not as talented and has to work extremely hard to contribute. Exceptionally gifted athletes often struggle with pride and cultivate an entitlement attitude. This reality is one reason that great players seldom become great coaches, whereas marginal players frequently become outstanding coaches. When I coached high school football and baseball, I became convinced that the players who benefited the most from athletics were those who barely made the team. I remember a particular football player who was the hardest worker in practice and in the weight room but who rarely ever stepped on the field. Years later when I see him, he always talks with delight about being a part of those teams and credits his football experience with helping him become successful in the workplace and as a father.

The call of the gospel to self-denial and the call of the culture to self-referential self-esteem are diametrically opposite messages. Christ calls his followers to decrease that he might increase (John 3:30), while the self-esteem mentality sees no purpose beyond the individual increasing. As our children participate in youth sports and other activities, opportunities for self-exaltation will be plentiful, and the temptation to shield our children from failure and adversity will be ever present. However, as Christian parents, our goal for our children must transcend momentary comfort and temporary happiness. Our discipleship must seek to make a biblical worldview and the gospel of Jesus Christ more intelligible to our children as they compete in sports. In order to achieve that goal, sports participation trophies will have no place of pride in our homes and we must fight for our children's right to lose.

Chapter Six

Sports and Safety

*For the sake of Christ, then, I am content
with weaknesses, insults, hardships,
persecutions, and calamities. For when
I am weak, then I am strong.*

(2 Corinthians 12:10)

H alf guru, half beast of burden," is how columnist Thomas Boswell once described baseball catchers.[1] Most baseball players simply don their uniform; but like football players, catchers gird themselves for battle. Resembling a medieval warrior, the catcher wears a protective mask and body armor that allude to the uniqueness of his responsibility on the baseball diamond. Herold "Muddy" Ruel of the Washington Senators in the 1920s, a lawyer turned catcher, was lovingly dubbed catcher's gear "the tools of ignorance"—a fitting name, only if you understand that the ignorance does not refer to intellectual capacity but to the audacity of willingly embracing such a burdensome and self-destructive task.

The Wise Men Who Wear the Tools of Ignorance

The indignity of the catcher's body armor and the inglorious squatting position he assumes about 150 times each game belies his vital role as field general. An effective catcher possesses simultaneously a vast array of mental and physical skills. Whereas most players react to what is happening in a baseball game, the catcher initiates and shapes virtually all action during the course of the game. As he relays signals to the pitcher, he is not simply concerned with a single pitch but how any given pitch will fit into the entire sequence of pitches throughout the game. Particularly gifted catchers possess a keen baseball intellect and lightning-fast judgment. His task calls him to understand the temper and ability of his pitcher. He must also be an expert in the tendencies of each hitter on the opposing team as well as the strike zone of the umpire that day. With every pitch, this armor-donning baseball guru must process information about the score, the inning, the count, the positioning of all the fielders, the base runners, and the strategic tendencies of the opposing manager while catching 90-mph fastballs and blocking sliders in the dirt.

An excellent catcher is a baseball savant, though his body often bears the scars of a rough-hewn frontline combat soldier. Anyone who has ever shaken the hand of a man who spent a couple of decades catching is reminded that he paid a price to play the position. A former catcher's fingers are usually described with words like "gnarly," "disjointed," and "twisted." His hands often look as though they possess several thumbs. The beast of burden's well-worn exterior disguises his aptitude as a baseball chess master. Catchers are brutish but graceful, stout but quick, rugged but able to delicately frame a pitch—field generals but also competent psychologists. It is not at all surprising that former catchers are more likely to become Major League managers than any other position player.

So many things about baseball exhibit nearly perfect tension. Famed sportswriter Red Smith once said, "Ninety feet between bases is perhaps as close as man has ever come to perfection." Everything is so perfectly calibrated: the pitcher stands 60-feet, 6-inches from the catcher, the bases and home plate are 90 feet apart, and outfield fences are just close enough to make home runs a constant possibility but far enough away so they do not dominate the game. The result is an almost mathematically precise competitive balance on every pitch and play. Baseball is not a collision sport; it is patient and measured with sudden bursts of intense action and is occasionally punctuated by a collision—usually involving the catcher at home plate.

A catcher who is doing his job well will largely go unnoticed, but there is one moment when a baseball catcher has historically had every eye riveted. The catcher is charged with the responsibility to protect the most sacred spot in the baseball universe, that irregular pentagon with two parallel sides called home plate. Bart Giamatti asserted that baseball is a narrative epic about going home and how hard it is to get there.[2] The catcher must position himself to receive from a fielder the urgently hurled ball while preparing himself for a potentially savage collision. Courage and toughness are daily demands on a catcher, but blocking home plate from an adrenaline-filled base-running missile is his seminal moment of truth—the hit, the catch, the throw, the runner, the catcher, impact, and a cloud of dust. Leaning in as closely as he can without getting demolished himself, the umpire holds his call to see if the catcher held onto the ball. With every eye fixated on baseball's ground zero, a breathless stadium waits for seconds that seem like hours, and the umpire finally makes the call. The stadium exhales with either joy or grief.

For 150 years of baseball, home plate collisions were considered good, clean, hard baseball; extremely rare, but a part of the game. They have been a part of the (almost) perfect competitive balance found in the sport. Home plate is utterly unique from all of the other bases because the runner does not need to possess it to score safely. A fleeting second of contact by any portion of his anatomy or attire with that disputed white rubber pentagon before being tagged, and he is welcomed home in celebration by his teammates. The runner's advantage of only having to touch, not possess, home plate is countered by allowing catchers who possess the ball to defend the plate. He cannot block the plate without the baseball, for the Major League Baseball rulebook states, "The catcher, without the ball in his possession, has no right to block the pathway of the runner attempting to score. The base line belongs to the runner and the catcher should be there only when he is fielding a ball or when he already has the ball in his hand" (7.06b).

Peter Morris argues that the baseball catcher emerged as an iconic American hero because he embodied the traits Americans most revered: courage, resourcefulness, and extraordinary skill in a specific task. Morris explains, "His rise to prominence occurred simply because he was able to resolve the long list of contradictory requirements that had thwarted earlier prospective heroes." Morris contends that because of catchers' skill and courageous toughness, they became "American folk heroes in the tradition of frontiersmen, mountain men, and cowboys."[3] The catcher's bravery when blocking home plate at risk of personal injury provided young men an inspiring flesh-and-blood stalwart of self-sacrificial toughness. He was not the initiator of violence but equal to the task when the violence came.

The quintessentially American game rarely changes anything that would tamper with the essential character of the game (the American League designated hitter rule in 1973 being one exception).[4] Baseball is a game of tradition and relishes its continuity with the past. If a baseball fan from a century ago were dropped in a Major League Baseball park today, some things would surprise him. However, unlike other professional sports, he would have no problem following the game. Nevertheless, in the name of safety, Major League Baseball voted to tamper with the character of the game by banning collisions at home plate in 2014 (MLB Rulebook 7.13). In my opinion, the ban is unnecessary and removes some of the glorious mystique of the half guru, half beast of burden whom we call a baseball catcher.

When the topic of injury-producing home plate collisions arises, several scenes come to mind: the Pete Rose and Ray Fosse All-Star game collision in 1970; the 1987 collision when Bo Jackson steamrolled Rick

Dempsey at the plate; and more recently, the 2011 collision between Scott Cousins and Buster Posey, which resulted in a broken leg for the catcher. There have been other home plate collisions resulting in injury, but what is most noticeable is how infrequently injuries occur. The catcher is in more danger from 95-mph foul tips consistently careening off his catcher's mask than he is from home plate collisions. The Rose collision that hampered Fosse's career is the most infamous, but it is important to note that the immediate reaction to the incident was praise for Rose's hustle and both players' toughness. Rose also had to have medical attention as a result of the collision. The American League team's manager, Earl Weaver, responded to the play by asserting, "I thought Rose got there a little ahead of the ball, and Fosse was trying to block the plate. They did what they had to do." Rose and Fosse both spoke out in vigorous opposition to the home plate collision ban when it was proposed.

What changed? Baseball did not significantly change, but we have. Our contemporary safety-centric worldview counts bravery and courage as vices not virtues. *Merriam-Webster* defines *courage* as "the ability to do something that you know is difficult or dangerous." Courage is not the absence of fear, but rather is acting on the premise that there is something more important than fear. Whether or not you agree with me about the wrongness of banning home plate collisions, I think most would agree that courage demands a dose of danger. Our current cultural cult of safety treats willingly pursuing a difficult or dangerous task as foolish, sinful even—not heroic. G. K. Chesterton argues, "Courage is almost a contradiction in terms. It means a strong desire to live taking the form of a readiness to die. 'He that will lose his life, the same shall save it', [Matt. 16:25]." Genuine Christian courage, according to Chesterton, combines "a strong desire for living with a strange carelessness about dying."[5] Recklessness and self-protecting safety both have the same sinful root: self-centeredness. A culture where everyone values safety first is a very dangerous place to live. Biblically, safety is not a virtue, but self-sacrificial courage certainly is. I think we were wiser when we rightly appreciated men who would courageously take up "the tools of ignorance" and risk safety to defend "home" for the sake of their team.

The Danger of Making the Gridiron Too Safe

Contact and collision in baseball is occasional, whereas in football, controlled, repetitive hits and human pileups are a part of the game. There is little doubt that football has become America's favorite sporting obsession. Football games are huge events where fans dress up, chant, cheer, and tailgate. Even though a football team only has a handful of home games each season, the atmosphere and pageantry of football attracts countless people who are fans of the spectacle, even though they know very little of the nuances of the zone read, Tampa 2 coverage, or the wing-bone offense. No other game combines brute force and elegant choreography the way football does. To borrow David Foster Wallace's terminology, football is "Mozart and Metallica at the same time, and the harmony is exquisite."[6]

But with our safety-centric cultural ethos, there are those who question the moral acceptability of a physically combative sport like football. They consider the game barbaric or a blood sport. Author Malcolm Gladwell has called for the abolition of college football. He refers to football as the human version of dogfighting.[7] In a January 27, 2013 interview with the *New Republic*, President Barack Obama was quoted as saying, "I'm a big football fan, but I have to tell you, if I had a son, I'd have to think long and hard before I let him play football." In 2013, Christian theologian and personal friend Owen Strachan wrote an article called, "Our Shaken Faith in Football," which addresses the question, "Should Christian fans step away from such a physically devastating, violent sport?"[8]

The question of whether football is too violent to be deemed ethically acceptable is not a new one. In 1905, the game was far more violent and brutal than today— eighteen men died on the college football field, which led then Harvard president Charles Eliot to describe the game as having "barbarous ethics" worse than "cockfighting" and to call for the abolition of football on college campuses. In response, President Theodore Roosevelt described such an attitude as foolish and stated his concern about producing "mollycoddles instead of vigorous men." Roosevelt said, "I believe in rough games and in rough, manly sports" and asserted he had no intention of allowing Eliot to "emasculate football."[9] He committed himself to doing everything he could to save football. His efforts resulted in a few changes that rescued the manly game he loved.

Roosevelt had been a football fan since he was an eighteen-year-old Harvard freshman and witnessed his first game in 1876 against rival Yale. He was a war hero in the 1880s and 1890s and led the Rough Riders to military victory in Cuba. While recruiting men for the Rough Riders, he looked for those who had been cowboys, ranchers, and football players. In a speech urging men to live a strenuous life, he said, "In short, in life, as in a football game, the principle to follow is: hit the line hard; don't foul and don't shirk, but hit the line hard!"[10] In *The Big Scrum: How Teddy Roosevelt Saved Football*, John J. Miller writes, "In Roosevelt's estimation, the foes of football were wrongheaded idealists who simply refused to accept the risks that are attached to virtually any human endeavor. They threatened to feminize an entire generation."[11]

Roosevelt's willingness to listen to concerns, but his ultimate defense of a brand of football far more brutish and violent than today, is instructive for the contemporary conversation about the ethics of the combat sport. We should always be willing to reform the game in ways that reduce risk but do not destroy the very character of the physical and manly sport. For instance, in 2013, the National Football League reached a $765 million settlement with 4,500 former players seeking damages from the NFL for concealing the long-term damages of concussion-related injuries. Research shows that repeated hits to the head are linked to chronic traumatic encephalopathy (CTE), a degenerative brain disease that can result in mood disorders and dementia. The NFL certainly does have an ethical responsibility to inform players embarking on a professional football career of the existing data and potential dangers related to a career in the game and ought to be held accountable when they neglect that duty.

Nevertheless, it is wrongheaded to use data from NFL football players who have made the game their career at the highest level and attribute it to everyone who plays football. An estimated 3.9 million people participate in playing football in America each year, and of that number only 68,000 participate on the college level and 1,696 are on NFL rosters. More than 95 percent of the people who participate in tackle football are under eighteen years of age. There is a qualitative difference between playing youth football and playing in the National Football League. However, despite the logical difference, many American parents are keeping their children out of youth football. According to an annual survey by the National Federation of State High School Associations, more than 25,000 fewer children played football in the US in 2012 than only four years before. This is tragic.

Recent studies about extreme long-term running published in the medical journal *Mayo Clinic Proceedings* concluded, "Long-term excessive endurance exercise may induce pathological structural remodeling of the heart and large arteries . . . [and] excessive exercise significantly increases mortality."[12] In other words, new research suggests that long-term competitive running at extreme levels may damage one's health and has a relationship to heart disease and premature death. If this research were taken to argue that youth physical fitness programs, which emphasized running, were dangerous and should be avoided because of potential heart problems, that would be an illogical and wrongheaded overreaching application of the data. It is akin to arguing that health concerns about repeated head trauma of college and professional football players means that youth football is dangerous and should be avoided.

A March 2012 study by the National Institute for Occupational Safety and Health found that NFL players are living longer than men in the general population.[13] They had a much lower rate of cancer-related deaths, and the risk of dying from heart disease or suicide was also lower than that of the general population. The primary area of concern was that NFL players had a greater risk of death involving neurodegenerative causes than that of the general population (still less than one percent of the players studied). As Daniel Flynn, author of *War on Football*, explains, "On the whole, people who play football are going to walk away from the game healthier than the people who sit in the stands and watch it."[14]

As we normally reckon safety, football is a safe activity and it is getting safer. In the 1960s there was an average of about twenty-five football-related deaths a season. The average in recent years is around four. Every death is tragic and the death of a young person bears a unique pain, but the risk of experiencing a football-related fatality is remarkably low. To provide some perspective, in 2011 there were twice as many cyclists treated for head injuries than football players and ninety-one cycling fatalities under twenty years of age as compared to four on the football field. In the September 5, 2011 edition of the *Houston Chronicle*, Dr. Gary Brock, who specializes in pediatric surgery asserts, "We see more catastrophic injuries among cheerleaders than among any group of athletes. . . . The risk per hour of activity is seven times greater than with other participatory sports. . . . I tell parents that it's safer to send their children to Pop Warner (football), than to the playground."[15]

There are inevitable risks tied to every human endeavor. In fact, according to a study done from 1982–2012 by the National Center for Catastrophic Sport Injury Research, cheerleading is seven times more dangerous for catastrophic injury than any other high school sport, but it is certainly worth the risk as well.[16] We are right to count the cost, but we must also be concerned about the negative consequences of a safety-above-all worldview. Laziness and intentional under-achievement, along with a safety-centric worldview, are enemies to the advancement of the gospel. Likewise, there is a price to pay on the football field for laziness and lack of focus. Football represents one of the only major American institutions still standing that speaks unashamedly about manliness and toughness. Boys are drawn to demanding physical competition against other boys, assertive male leadership, and a cause that demands sacrifice and calculated risk. These are good things that ought to be cultivated on a pathway from boyhood to Christian manhood.

Courage and calculated risk-taking are casualties of our contemporary safety-centric worldview. Sadly, evangelicals seem to be leading the movement to train bravery and adventure out of our children in favor of a cult of safety. Children, who are virtually bubble wrapped by their parents to ride bikes in the front yard and do not participate in things like football or cheerleading because they might get hurt, will have a difficult time finding Paul remotely intelligible when he asserts, "For I am ready not only to be imprisoned but even to die in Jerusalem for the name of the Lord Jesus" (Acts 21:13).

Anthony Esolen has noted that football uniquely stirs the passions and intellectual interest of boys and men because it speaks the sacrificial language of men in a way the contemporary church often misses. He writes, "A true man, and there are many still, struggling to be both true and man, would sooner have his right arm wither than to change loyalty to the Pittsburgh Steelers. Yet he leaves the church. Why? Sin, of course; but in fact the Pittsburgh Steelers present themselves as more worthy of loyalty than does a church that demands nothing."[17]

I am certainly not defending everything that surrounds our modern American infatuation with football. I am saddened every time a player gets injured on the football field, but no more so than when one is injured in a cycling or skateboarding accident. Nevertheless, Roosevelt was wise when he recruited men who had played football for his Rough Riders military unit. Perhaps the church would be strengthened by a few more ministers of the gospel who have served in the military, played football, or sweated in the fields of a farm. We need to be reminded that we do not simply surrender our intellect to Christ, we surrender our very selves, including our bodies. Our Christian worldview and ethics are compatible with a proving ground like football. The church is always in need of Christian Rough Riders who are willing to serve the church self-sacrificially and enter spiritual battle, no matter the cost. The modern church has too many mollycoddles instead of vigorous Christians, and our mission demands the latter.

Safe Parenting or Christian Parenting

As culture obsesses over how to remove any and every risk of danger from sports, it seems the modern American evangelical parenting manifesto follows a similar track: be nice, be happy, and be safe—no matter what. The problem is that none of those assertions represent distinctive Christian values. Of all the names people called Jesus in the Bible, never once was he referred to as nice or safe. Jesus was described as one who speaks with authority, a madman, a glutton, a blasphemer, a sinner, and as one who acted by demonic power. Jesus did not cozy up comfortably with the wisdom of the world, but rather turned the wisdom of the world upside down. In an age of helicopter parenting, Christian parents should know better than to hover constantly over their children in a vain attempt to mitigate all risk from their lives. Living life involves inevitable risk; Christian parents must teach their children to take self-sacrificial, calculated risks for the glory of Christ and the good of others. One excellent context for teaching these Christian values is the athletic field.

Safety is far less important than Christ-exalting bravery and courage. Parents must intentionally train their children toward both physical and moral courage. According to biblical wisdom, laziness is not just a physical problem; it is a spiritual one and represents a life of wickedness and folly. The mother or father who is satisfied with having a nice child who makes good grades but sleeps until noon and does very little in the way of sacrificially serving the family and others is parenting a fool (Prov. 6:6–11; 21:25; 26:13–16). Christian parents should see sports as one tool they can use to defy the spirit of the age by teaching children bravery and cruciform ambition. As C. S. Lewis helpfully explains, "Courage is not simply *one* of the virtues, but the form of every virtue at the testing point, which means, at the point of highest reality. A chastity or honesty or mercy which yields to danger will be chaste or honest or merciful only on conditions. Pilate was merciful till it became risky."[18]

I fear that in the name of nice, happy, and safe children many Christian families are practically abandoning "the faith that was once for all delivered to the saints" (Jude 3). Affirming the gospel message with our lips but parenting on a daily basis as if nothing is more important than personal safety and our immediate well-being will have disastrous consequences. Adults who believe life is about being nice, happy, and safe do not joyfully commit their lives to courageously take the gospel to their neighborhood or to the ends of the earth (Acts 5:41–42). Making it our life goal to shield our children from all discomfort and any and every form of danger will only serve to make Christ's call unintelligible.

Courageous Conviction vs. Safe Sentimentality

Trading courage for sentimentality is tragic, not simply for individuals, but for the society as well. To a disturbing degree, the Christian community has been seduced by sentimentality, which is the desire to have Christian convictions that cost nothing and for which there is no need to suffer. Christian sentimentality trivializes the truth and transforms the call to spiritual war into self-referential religious therapy. Simply put, if the gospel is true, Christian sentimentality is a lie. Paul tells Timothy, "Therefore do not be ashamed of the testimony about our Lord, nor of me his prisoner, but share in suffering for the gospel by the power of God" (2 Tim. 1:8) and, "All who desire to live a godly life in Christ Jesus will be persecuted" (2 Tim. 3:12). A world in which nothing is worth suffering and dying for is a world where it is difficult to discern what is worth living for. Sports competition by nature is unsentimental. It consistently provides doses of stark reality: victory or defeat, success or failure, self-sacrifice or self-protection, determination or vacillation. These nonnegotiable realities, when squarely faced, call for humility and leave little room for self-adulation. Overvaluing safety above these vital lessons is selfish, shortsighted, and dangerous in its own ignoble way.

Chapter Seven

Sports and the Church

But as it is, God arranged the members in the
body, each one of them, as he chose. If all were
a single member, where would the body be?
As it is, there are many parts, yet one body.

(1 Corinthians 12:18–20)

After decades serving in ministry, there is rarely a day that goes by that I do not reflect on how thankful I am for the training I have received for pastoral ministry. I am thankful that, as a new Christian, I was shaped by the expository sermons of Pastor Greg Belser at Morningview Baptist Church. After professing a call to ministry, I received encouragement and guidance from my pastor, Thom Rainer, at Green Valley Baptist Church. I had the privilege of excellent seminary training at Southwestern Baptist Theological Seminary and The Southern Baptist Theological Seminary. However, there is something else that has been most beneficial for the day-to-day grind of pastoral leadership and decision making as a shepherd of a local church. I am thinking of the lessons I have learned through sports about leadership, courage, running a program, building team chemistry, communicating a big-picture vision, teaching fundamentals, handling criticism, discipline, motivation, and inspiration.

Like Paul, I cannot think about my Christian walk without noting the obvious parallels to lessons learned from athletic competition. There are some important and practical life lessons that are best learned in the hot sun and heat of conflict from someone who cares more about the goal that brought the team together than any individual's feelings. I, and countless others, have been shaped for the good of the church by our sports experiences. I will share a few examples from my own life in the hope that my experiences will trigger some for you or help you to think about being more intentional as you participate in sports and guide your children who are involved in sports.

Coach Mitchell, Baseball, and the Beauty of Sacrifice

Coach Wayne Mitchell was not simply the head baseball coach at Robert E. Lee High School in Montgomery, Alabama; he was a local baseball institution. Coach Mitchell taught the game down to the most seemingly insignificant and minute details. We had lessons in how to put our baseball cap on our heads (always front to back), how to wear our uniforms, and how to run onto the field. Coach Mitchell had attended Robert E. Lee High School as a student and excelled on the baseball team. In 1964, Mitchell graduated from Lee and enrolled at Huntington College, where he was a star left-handed pitcher. As a freshman, he went 5-0 with a 1.00 ERA, and when he graduated, he held the school record for career victories.

After college, he became an assistant baseball coach at Robert E. Lee from 1971–1974. He left to become the head coach at Huntington College from 1975–1978 and then returned to Robert E. Lee as the head baseball coach in 1980. When I was playing Dixie Youth baseball for the National League in Montgomery as a young boy, I dreamed of wearing that distinctive "L" emblazoned on a fire-red baseball cap for Robert E. Lee and playing for Coach Mitchell. I vividly remember the thrill of putting on that Robert E. Lee High School baseball uniform for the first time in 1984. I did not know it at the time because he never talked about it, but in 1978 Mitchell had been diagnosed with cancer. In January 1986, my senior year, Mitchell began experimental cancer treatments that prevented him from being with the team. Coach Jim Arrington had the unenviable task of filling in for a local baseball coaching legend that season. Our team prayed for Coach at every practice, and on two occasions I visited him in his home with one of my teammates. On those visits he would not talk about himself, but he lit up when he talked about the team.

Mitchell was a Christian, and the authenticity of his faith was evident in the way he coached baseball and the way he persevered in the face of cancer. He could be stern, like the day he told me to decide whether I wanted to be a rock star or a baseball player. He assured me that, if my choice was a baseball player, I should get my hair cut. I knew it was a command, not a request. He was a walking encyclopedia of baseball knowledge and strategy, but it was evident that coaching high school baseball was far more to him than a way to earn a living. I did not think about it this way at the time, but reflecting back, I think that he saw baseball as his mission field. I am not suggesting he was overtly evangelistic, because he was not. I think he saw coaching baseball as a vital way he served Christ. He never made it back to the baseball field, dying shortly after the 1986 baseball season.

To say that I was not very reflective as a high school student and athlete would be an understatement. I had always cherished baseball, and Coach Mitchell knew as much about the game as anyone I had ever met, so I listened to everything he said. Three years after graduating high school, I became a Christian while following in Mitchell's footsteps playing baseball at Huntington College. Not until then did I realize just how much Mitchell had impacted me. It was common for me to be in a Bible study and link what I was learning to life lessons Mitchell had taught me on the baseball field. I would hear his voice in my head and began to understand that he had been teaching me more than baseball. Below are a few of the lessons that Coach Mitchell taught me through the game of baseball.

Winning by Routine Plays

One of Coach Mitchell's mantras was that baseball games are not won or lost by spectacular plays but by routine plays. He said that everybody loves the home run, the strikeout, and the diving catch, but plenty of players can do all of those things who make too many mistakes on routine plays. He drilled into our heads that playing time was dependent upon consistency and making the routine plays. When Paul exhorts the church at Colossae, "And whatever you do, in word or deed, do everything in the name of the Lord Jesus, giving thanks to God the Father through him" (Col. 3:17), he is calling for the routine and nonspectacular to be redeemed to the glory of Christ. We are called to have an earthy spirituality that embraces instead of begrudges the everydayness of life. A radical commitment to Christ manifests itself in the ordinary plodding of loving God and neighbor in daily life. The turning point of a baseball game is often something that did not seem overly significant at the time. Life is similar. We should repent of thinking we can decide what the really big moments in life are and simply live to glorify God in our daily routine.

The Beauty of Sacrifice

Coach Mitchell believed that one of the most beautiful plays in baseball was a sacrifice. I can still hear him saying, "If someone hits a home run or makes a diving play, I don't care what you do. But, if someone lays down a sacrifice bunt or hits a sacrifice fly to move a runner over, then you better be out of that dugout cheering them when they return." Bunting is one of those non-glamorous jobs that looks easy from a distance but is far from easy in reality. Sacrificing runners into scoring position is out of favor with some modern sabermetrics baseball stat addicts, but I consider it a beautiful and vital part of the game. Baseball is a fundamentally communal sport where the goal is to get runs across the plate and help the team score. In fact, even in statistical analysis most baseball fans value runs-batted-in over personal runs scored. The value of sacrificing to help score runs is woven into the very fabric of the game.

On the baseball diamond with Coach Mitchell, I began to understand something of the importance of sacrifice for a cause bigger than the individual before I ever came to saving faith in Christ. When I read that "while we were still sinners, Christ died for us" (Rom. 5:8) and that Jesus told his disciples, "If anyone would come after me, let him deny himself and take up his cross and follow me" (Matt. 16:24), I could not help but remember those lessons. Coach Mitchell taught us about sacrifice. The first time I read the great missionary William Carey's (1761–1834) words about his self-sacrificial gospel ministry in India, "I can plod. I can persevere in any definite pursuit. To this I owe everything," I remembered Coach Mitchell telling us about the beauty of sacrifice and to focus on daily consistency and making the routine plays. I thought, *I may not be able to hit a lot of home runs in my Christian walk, but I can learn to sacrifice daily in Jesus' name.* I could live out the sacrificial vision Paul advocated when he wrote, "To the weak I became weak, that I might win the weak. I have become all things to all people, that by all means I might save some" (1 Cor. 9:22).

Passing on the Legacy

Coach Mitchell probably assumed that he wasn't making much of an impact on me at the time he was my coach. I could have been voted least likely to become a pastor in my high school class. One of the most embarrassing moments of my high school years was the time Mitchell asked me to lead the team in quoting the Lord's Prayer at the end of practice. There was a moment of awkward silence that probably lasted five seconds, though it felt like five hours, until I said, "I'm sorry, Coach, but I don't know it." He quickly said, "No problem. I will lead us." Well, I do know the Lord and his model prayer now. In fact, by a miracle of God's grace, people now call me "Pastor." My love for the game of baseball and the influence of courageous and gracious men who also love the game, like Mitchell, have helped form and shape my life in profound ways.

I am thankful for the many lessons I have learned over the years on a baseball diamond. To me baseball is the greatest game. I have passed down to my three sons as I have tutored them in the great game many of the lessons I learned while playing the national pastime. My oldest son graduated high school twenty-nine years after my last season wearing a Robert E. Lee baseball uniform. I wish he could have met Coach Mitchell, but in a sense, he already has through the lessons from Coach that I have passed on to him. I am thankful for an excellent baseball coach who taught me about more than baseball. I think it would please him to know that I am still trying, as a Christian, to make the routine plays consistently, celebrate the beauty of sacrifice, and help my children and congregation to do the same.

Training to Serve the Church on the Gridiron

After I finished playing college baseball and graduated from Huntingdon College, I accepted a job teaching and coaching at McAdory High School in Birmingham, Alabama. What I learned coaching football alongside Coach David Powell has also proven invaluable to me as a pastor. I was amazed as I watched him help the players understand the unique ways they could individually contribute to the team's success. He taught me how to effectively communicate the priority of the team over the individual, but not to forget that the team was made up of unique individuals. Strategies and schemes were important but not ultimate. Coach Powell reminded us that we are coaching people, and it is people, not schemes, who make plays. More important than the game plan is getting the team to work as a self-sacrificial unit that trusts the plan and preparation, but most importantly, trusts each other and understands their need for one another.

Passionately Teaching People, Not Schemes

I once heard Urban Meyer, head football coach at Ohio State University, verbalize the kind of lessons I had learned from Coach Powell during a coaching clinic. (The following quotes are approximations based on my notes of the talks.)

> People think the content of what you teach—the scheme—wins games, but that's only about twenty percent. It is not just the scheme. If it was simply schemes, everybody would run the same thing. I don't care what we run. You can win with all kinds of schemes, but I do care that we passionately believe in what we run and teach the players to believe in it passionately.[1]

Meyer continued explaining his "no-excuses-teaching-people" approach to coaching:

> We teach our coaches to be direct teachers of people and not simply presenters. The difference

between a teacher and a presenter is this: a presenter presents information and if the student does not know it, they fail. Teachers exhaust all possible venues and resources to understand how the player learns in order to get the information across and to make sure that the player knows exactly what he is doing. A football coach must be a teacher and not a presenter because his teaching is getting evaluated every single week on the field. If he is simply a presenter, the moving vans will show up soon.[2]

For the Christian, these lessons and this way of thinking should have a familiar ring. The apostle Paul describes the church as a unified body with many interdependent parts bound together in a common mission:

> But as it is, God arranged the members in the body, each one of them, as he chose. If all were a single member, where would the body be? As it is, there are many parts, yet one body. The eye cannot say to the hand, "I have no need of you," nor again the head to the feet, "I have no need of you." . . . If one member suffers, all suffer together; if one member is honored, all rejoice together. Now you are the body of Christ and individually members of it. (1 Cor. 12:18–21, 26–27)

Paul also explains that the church is called to the passionate and direct teaching of the gospel to all people, exhausting all possible venues and resources in doing so. The church is not a disinterested presenter of the truth, indifferent to the outcome. To the contrary, Paul exhorts:

> For though I am free from all, I have made myself a servant to all, that I might win more of them. To the Jews I became as a Jew, in order to win Jews. To those under the law I became as one under the law (though not being myself under the law) that I might win those under the law. To those outside the law I became as one outside the law (not being outside the law of God but under the law of Christ) that I might win those outside the law. To the weak I became weak, that I might win the weak. I have become all things to all people, that by all means I might save some. I do it all for the sake of the gospel, that I may share with them in its blessings. (1 Cor. 9:19–23)

As Christian sports fans observe the passion, discipline, hard work, focus, and agonizing intensity of coaches and athletes in pursuit of what Paul refers to as a "crown that will fade away," we should naturally ask what it says about our pursuit of a "crown that will never fade away" (1 Cor. 9:25 HCSB; see also Rev. 2:10). The apostle Paul calls Christians to reorient every aspect of our thinking and lifestyle for the greatest cause in the cosmos of bringing the gospel to others. The Christian involved in athletics should pursue victory with self-sacrificial zeal to the glory of God, but that pursuit should be rightly understood as momentary and subordinate when compared to what is eternal and ultimate.

Consider the words of Horatius Bonar (1808–1889), a Scottish preacher and author, from his classic book *Words to Winners of Souls*:

> When we can rest satisfied with using the means for saving souls without seeing them really saved, or we ourselves being broken-hearted by it, and at the same time quietly talk of leaving the event to God's disposal, we make use of a truth to cover and excuse a falsehood; for our ability to leave the matter thus is not, as we imagine, the result of heart-submission to God, but of heart-indifference to the salvation of the souls we deal with. No, truly, if the heart is really set on such an end, it must gain that end or break in losing it.[3]

There is no room for Christian casualness or indifference regarding our shared gospel mission as followers of Christ.

Hopeful Discipline

Another significant ministry lesson I learned while coaching high school athletics was that of hopeful discipline. Whenever a player has a character problem on or off the field, the common knee-jerk reaction is almost always that the player should be immediately kicked off the team. Many consider the willingness to have a quick dismissal trigger a mark of a disciplined and clean sports program, and I would have probably agreed at one time. While it is true that some coaches will keep a talented player around simply because they want to win at all costs, some coaches' genuine concern about an individual player will produce a persistent patience often easily misconstrued as permissiveness by onlookers.

At McAdory High School we had a baseball player who was frequently in trouble. After several previous discipline situations, he was in trouble again for stealing from a concession stand during an away game. I assumed that the player would be immediately dismissed from the team. Instead, Coach Powell told the player that he had to turn in his uniform but would be able to get it back if he ran foul polls during the entirety of each practice session for a couple of months. Since the player was generally undisciplined, I assumed he would quit the team, but to my astonishment, he did not. He showed up every single day, did exactly what he was told to do, and eventually returned to the team. Coach Powell explained to me that this player came from a horrific home situation, and most people had already given up on him. However, he continued, we had a strategic opportunity to help him because baseball was one of the few things he really cared about.

Hopeful discipline is an excellent way to describe the responsibility of church members to hold one another accountable and practice congregational discipline. Remembrances of how we were stern with that young man and held him accountable but never lost hope have frequently come to mind in ministry. A church that ignores sin and fails to practice discipline in the congregation is not humble and loving but calloused and indifferent (Matt. 18:15–20; 1 Cor. 5:1–13; Gal. 6:1; Titus 3:9–11; James 5:19–20). The purpose of discipline in the church is never simply to punish; it is always a hopeful pursuit of repentance and restoration. Jesus says in Matthew 18:15, "If he listens to you, you have gained your brother," and Paul writes, "Brothers, if anyone is caught in any transgression, you who are spiritual should restore him in a spirit of gentleness. Keep watch on yourself, lest you too be tempted" (Gal. 6:1).

Nothing is more important than Christ and his church. We must hold tenaciously to biblical truth and standards, but we also must never lose sight of gospel hope. Our ultimate hope in the church is not in planning or programming but in the power of the gospel to transform any life: "For the word of the cross is folly to those who are perishing, but to us who are being saved it is the power of God" (1 Cor. 1:18). Have you ever noticed that even though the church at Corinth was an absolute mess, Paul refers to them as "God's church at Corinth . . . sanctified in Christ Jesus and called as saints" (1 Cor. 1:2 HCSB)? How can Paul be so hopeful? He maintained a gospel hope that refused to believe sin would have the final word. A person's sin and struggles (including our own) must never eclipse the power of the gospel in our hearts and minds.

Rickey, Robinson, Moral Courage, and the Church

Many of us have been blessed with coaches like Coach Mitchell and Coach Powell—people who have taught us life lessons that we have been able to apply to our walk with Christ and service to his church. Those who enjoy sports are also blessed with historical models and heroes as well. On April 15, 1947, Jackie Robinson, a twenty-eight-year-old rookie, courageously ran onto Ebbets Field, transforming one of the most sacred spaces in American culture by becoming the first black player in Major League Baseball. Robinson's number 42 has become sacred in Major League Baseball. On April 15, 1997, it became the only number retired throughout the entire league and it is prominently displayed in every Major League Park.

The recent lionization of Robinson as a significant hero of civil rights in America is heartening, but there is an oft-forgotten hero of the saga. Jackie Robinson and Branch Rickey, the Brooklyn Dodgers president who signed Robinson, were equally indispensable partners in what Rickey deemed "the great experiment." Rickey meticulously planned and shaped the master narrative for integrating the national pastime, but it could not have been accomplished without a unique player of great ability, personal courage, and unfathomable self-control. Rickey said of Robinson, "God was with me when I picked Jackie. I don't think any other man could have done what he did those first two or three years."[4] Robinson said that Rickey treated him "like a son"[5] and that Rickey was "a man blessed with true greatness."[6] It is reported that, at Rickey's funeral, Robinson said that he had done more for black Americans than any white man since Abraham Lincoln. Each man consistently gave the other full credit for bringing the integration of baseball to pass, which would forever change the nation for the good.

It is easy to miss the historical magnitude of that moment in 1947 for the advance of civil rights in America. All of Branch Rickey's advisers, close associates, family, and friends advised him against the move. He did it anyway. When Rickey petitioned Major League Baseball to allow him to integrate the league, the owners were opposed to his request. He did it anyway.

Consider that when Rickey signed Robinson to the Brooklyn Dodgers, breaking the color barrier in baseball, it was a year before President Truman ordered the United States military desegregated; seven years before the US Supreme Court rendered its decision in *Brown vs. Board of Education*; eight years before Rosa Parks refused to give up her seat on a Montgomery, Alabama, bus; ten years before President Eisenhower used the US military to enable the "Little Rock Nine" to attend Central High School in Arkansas; sixteen years before Martin Luther King Jr.'s "I Have a Dream" speech; seventeen years before the Civil Rights Act of 1964; and eighteen years before the Voting Rights Act of 1965.

Make first things first, seek the kingdom of God, and make yourself an example

Looking back on his role in the integration of baseball, Robinson concluded, "I must tell you that it was Mr. Rickey's drama and that I was only a principal actor."[7] Robinson's overstated, self-deprecating observation helps us remember that breaking the color barrier in baseball did not begin with "the great experiment." Mr. Rickey's drama began with his family's Midwestern Christian roots. His father was described as a "pious, devout, religious man . . . a genuine New Testament Christian," and his mother is said to have taught Branch countless Scripture stories even before he could read.[8] Biographer Murray Polner describes Rickey as a conservative evangelical Christian whose religious faith was the decisive factor in his commitment to racial equality. Rickey would often repeat the family motto he learned as a child, "Make first things first, seek the Kingdom of God, and make yourself an example."[9]

In 1903, Rickey was the twenty-one-year-old head baseball coach at Ohio Wesleyan University when his Christian conviction collided head-on with his love for the great game. Charles Thomas was recruited by Rickey to play catcher and was the only black player on the team. OWU traveled to South Bend, Indiana, for a game against Notre Dame. When they arrived, the hotel clerk refused to allow Thomas to stay because of a whites-only policy. Rickey persuaded the hotel to allow Thomas to go to his room and later requested a cot. That evening Rickey found his catcher sobbing and rubbing his hands and arms convulsively while muttering, "It's my skin. If only I could wipe off the color they could see I am a man like everybody else!" Rickey told him to "Buck up!" and said, "We will beat this one day!", but later noted that he never felt so helpless and vowed at that time that he would do whatever he could to end such humiliation.[10] This was an audacious thought for a twenty-one-year-old baseball coach at a small Christian college.

Branch Rickey was a baseball man to the core. He loved the game from childhood. He played baseball in college and professionally for the St. Louis Browns. Rickey once told a reporter his goal in life was "to be both a consistent Christian and a consistent ballplayer."[11] By all accounts, he was successful in the former, but his professional playing career was less than stellar. He possessed a career batting average of .239 with three home runs in three seasons, and as a catcher he holds the record for allowing 13 stolen bases in a single nine-inning game. In ten years as a Major

League Baseball manager, Rickey accumulated a pedestrian 597 wins and 664 losses.

In 1926, Rickey moved exclusively into his role as a baseball executive, which would eventually lead to his induction in the baseball Hall of Fame. Rickey-led teams won four World Series championships in his twenty-nine years. He revolutionized baseball and gained a competitive edge over other clubs by his innovation of using farm clubs to develop players for the big league club. Rickey was known as a Bible-quoting, tight-fisted Republican, a fierce competitor, and a shrewd negotiator whom players referred to as "El Cheapo." It was said that Rickey's everyday speech resembled a sermon, and second baseman Eddie Stanky once retorted after negotiating his contract with Rickey, "I got a million dollars' worth of free advice and a very small raise."[12]

A man can play baseball as a call of God

As an executive for the St. Louis Cardinals, Rickey unsuccessfully pushed for an end to segregated seating at the park and tested the waters for racial integration of the team but feared that a premature attempt in the wrong place would set back the cause. When Rickey left the Cardinals for the Brooklyn Dodgers in 1942, he immediately took the initiative to integrate baseball. The cultural moment and the location of the Dodgers in Brooklyn made it an opportune time for Rickey to act. Americans of all races were fighting in World War II against racist ideology in Europe while racist Jim Crow laws were in place back home. The tragic irony was slowly becoming apparent to many Americans. In Brooklyn, Rickey was in a place where he could make a credible case to ownership of potential profits if they were the first club to sign black players. Rickey used his business acumen to serve his conviction that segregation was morally indefensible. Rickey said, "I believe a man can play baseball as coming to him from a call of God."[13] Looking back on Rickey's life and legacy, one would have to conclude that he viewed being a baseball executive as a call of God as well.

In March 1945, Branch Rickey met at Joe's restaurant with Red Barber, the beloved Dodgers broadcaster, to tell him of his plan to sign a black man to play for the Dodgers. Barber was initially appalled but recalls Rickey telling him that he had to act because he had heard Charles Thomas crying for forty-one years. At that time, he did not know who that player would be, but later that summer scouts had narrowed the list down to a handful of players. It seems the initial plan was to sign several players at once, but instead, Rickey settled on Jackie Robinson. Biographer Jimmy Breslin asserts that Rickey broke the color line in baseball because "he thought it was God's work" and describes it as "the single most important act in the history of this nation."[14]

There is nobody on our side—Let's do it

In their first meeting, August 28, 1945, Rickey stunned Robinson with the news that he wanted him to play for the Brooklyn Dodgers. He grilled him for hours and made him commit to three years of non-retaliation. Rickey read to him from Giovanni Papini's book *Life of Christ* and pointed him to the biblical account of Jesus' Sermon on the Mount. Rickey told Robinson, "We can't fight our way through this, Robinson. We've got no army. There's virtually nobody on our side. No owners.

No umpires. Very few newspapermen. And I'm afraid many fans will be hostile. We'll be in a tough position. We can win only if we convince the world that I'm doing this because you are a great ball player and a fine gentleman."[15]

Rickey believed that the right player who was also the right person—full of moral courage and willing to commit to non-retaliation for three years—could end what he called an "odious injustice."[16] Rickey said about signing Robinson, "I couldn't face my God much longer knowing that His black creatures are held separate and distinct from His white creatures in the game that has given me all I own."[17] There is a sense in which two Christian men, Rickey and Robinson, laid out an incipient strategy that would be later utilized by Martin Luther King Jr. in the larger civil rights movement. Hank Aaron explains the symbolic power of Robinson in a Brooklyn Dodgers uniform when he writes that his father always set him straight when he talked about becoming a pilot or a baseball player by saying, "Ain't no colored pilots" and "Ain't no colored ballplayers," but after they sat at Hartwell Field and saw Robinson play an exhibition game in a Dodgers uniform, he never said it again.[18]

Rickey and Robinson: Baseball's Ferocious *Christian* Gentlemen

In his excellent biography on Branch Rickey, Lee Lowenfish describes him in the subtitle as "Baseball's Ferocious Gentleman." What an apt and powerful description. He was ferocious. Journalist John Chamberlain described Rickey as "one of the slyest men who ever lived, but in all fundamentals, a man of honor."[19] He was passionately driven to succeed and made no apologies for turning a profit in the process. Yet, his aggression and fierceness were guided by his Christian conviction and worldview. His life embodied Jesus' admonition to his disciples, sheep in the midst of wolves, to "be wise as serpents and innocent as doves" (Matt. 10:16).

On November 13, 1965, Branch Rickey stepped to the podium to speak after having been inducted into the Missouri Sports Hall of Fame. Baseball's ferocious gentleman had left the hospital against the advice of his doctors because, as he often said, "It is better to die ten minutes sooner than to live doing nothing."[20] He rose to speak about a topic he had lived: courage. He spoke of having objectives on which there is no price and began to tell the biblical story of Zaccheus, who he said "had the greatest amount of courage of any man in the Bible." He did not get to finish telling about one of his favorite biblical characters because, while still speaking, he collapsed and, less than a month later, died.[21]

Perhaps adding one word to Lowenfish's descriptive title of Rickey would prove helpful in thinking about both Rickey and Robinson: Baseball's Ferocious *Christian* Gentlemen. However, I fear that the moniker "Ferocious Christian Gentlemen" sounds oxymoronic in contemporary Christian circles where God is envisioned as a kind of cosmic smiley face and where Christian discipleship is cheapened to generic niceness. Too many Christians pursue comfort and respectability in the place of self-sacrificial "great experiments" that demand ferocious Christian gentlemen. Martin Luther King Jr. once said to Don Newcombe, "You'll never know what you and Jackie and Roy [Campanella] did to make it possible to do my job."[22] Billy Graham said of Branch Rickey, "He was a man of deep piety and integrity—that rare combination of a 'man's man' and a Christian man, at the same time."[23] Here's hoping Graham is wrong and the combination is not so rare, because our churches are in desperate need of some ferocious *Christian* gentlemen and gentlewomen, too.

Persevering Courage Precedes Moral Victory

As we have seen, all athletic competition demands a measure of courage. The possibility of failure is ever present, but in the face of it, the coach, athlete, or team must persist. The persevering courage in the face of failure and criticism that we often find in the pursuit of temporal championships in sporting competition should both challenge and encourage us as we pursue what is eternal. All leadership is comprised of essentially moral acts that demand courage. Leaders do not simply take a group of people as far as they are willing to go. Leaders call people to follow a path that they would not ordinarily take. Leadership is not a self-protective act because the leader must step away from the crowd, assert a vision, and call others to follow, not knowing how those he is leading will respond. Following Christ demands a willingness among his followers to lead in countless ways to the glory of God. In light of all the resources we have in Christ, the church ought to be the place where persevering self-sacrificial courage and bold leadership is most graphically on display.

Nick Saban, football coach at the University of Alabama, constantly tells his players, "Be where your feet are." In other words, be personally, emotionally,

and intellectually present in the physical place where
your feet are at every moment. He doesn't want his
team's focus to be what will happen if they get to the
national championship game but instead about what
they're doing that day to get better and positively impact
the team. Branch Rickey said, "I may not be able to do
something about racism in every field, but I can sure do
something about it in baseball."[24] Rickey was committed to being where his feet were for Christ, and he and
Robinson made a lasting culture-shaping difference.
The church must challenge its members to commit
themselves to the reality that our lives constitute our
unique, strategic gospel opportunity. Our interest in
sports can be instructive and spur us on toward faithfulness in the church of Jesus Christ.

Conclusion

The end of the matter; all has been heard.
Fear God and keep his commandments,
for this is the whole duty of man.

(Ecclesiastes 12:13)

I was a nineteen-year-old student playing college baseball when I put my faith in Jesus Christ as my Lord and Savior. In an instant, the entire course of my life changed, and I began rethinking every aspect of my life. Sports had always been a part of my day-to-day life, but now I wondered if that should continue to be the case. How was I to think about sports as a Christian? Were sports simply a waste of time that distracted me from really serving Jesus? Should I view sports as a guilty pleasure? Or could my interest and involvement in sports serve as a context in which I honored Jesus and challenged others with a similar interest to do the same? I wrestled with all these questions as a new believer.

Twenty-eight years later much has changed. I am the married father of eight children, a pastor, and a seminary professor with a Masters of Divinity and a

PhD in theology. In this book you have read my attempts to answer those earlier questions. These answers have not been formulated as abstract and detached ideas, but rather they have been developed in the context of my deepest passions as a shepherd of my family and the church and as a teacher of future shepherds and missionaries, who happens to enjoy sports. As I speak on these matters, I feel the weight of responsibility to be biblically faithful, Christ-centered, and gospel-focused. I have a clear conscience as I assert that a Christian can enjoy sports to the glory of God, but I am also sure that cannot happen without an intentional commitment to do so.

C. S. Lewis described humanity in his classic *Mere Christianity* in the following way: "God made us: invented us as a man invents an engine. A car is made to run on gasoline, and it would not run properly on anything else. Now God designed the human machine to run on Himself." He continued, "God cannot give us a happiness and peace apart from Himself, because it is not there. There is no such thing." He concluded that the sin and corruption in the world was the result of people and institutions "trying to run it on the wrong juice."[1]

Every part of our lives, including our sports lives, must run on "the right juice" or we will inevitably turn gifts into idols. To run on the right juice, we must forsake a self-referential approach to life, embracing a radically Christ-centered life and walking humbly before God with fierce gospel-focused intentionality before man in community. When sports are not approached with intentional Christ-centeredness, they are corrupted and can easily become a curse rather than a blessing. Sports are not inherently good in a fallen world. Like all things, sports must be redeemed and renewed in light of the gospel of Jesus Christ.

A Biblical Framework for Christian Engagement with Sports

Below is my attempt to provide a biblical framework for a Christian engagement with sports. This constitutes the framework that has driven the theological and practical conclusions in the book. I summarize the framework here in hopes that these headings with brief explanations will provide the reader with a convenient place to review. Also, it is important to note that when I speak of sport in general terms, I do not intend that all activities done under the banner of sports are validated or that all expressions of sports activity are permissible without boundaries. To the contrary, sports, like all else, must be evaluated in relation to God's revelation in the Bible, and every thought must be taken captive to obey Christ.

Some Christians would do well to remember that God does not only save our brains, he redeems our bodies as well. Paul exhorts, "I appeal to you therefore, brothers, by the mercies of God, to present your bodies as a living sacrifice, holy and acceptable to God, which is your spiritual worship" (Rom. 12:1). The believer is set apart to God as a unified whole, consisting of both soul and physical body. The desires of the redeemed spirit are carried out bodily, and the same will be true in the consummated kingdom of Christ without the presence of sin. In the new heaven and new earth, all aspects of creation and culture will be redeemed. Imagine technology, artistry, relationships, construction, work, and play, enjoyed apart from the presence of sin. These cultural realities, like sports, will be present, but they will be even more enjoyable than they are now. We will not serve and worship God in heaven as disembodied spirits but with resurrected bodies. Our enjoyment of the new heavens and new earth will know no limits as we reign with him over his new creation. We will have things to do, places to go, people to see, and I certainly believe we will hear, "Play ball!" and for that I say "Amen!"

Sports are . . .

A gift of God

Thus, sports are a nonessential but inevitable response of God's image bearers to his creative order and design that serves his command that his creatures take dominion under his authority, by enhancing human gifts and skills through competitive interaction.

A manifestation of cultural rootedness

Thus, sports are a manifestation of culture-making, which reminds God's image bearers of his providential kindness in their rootedness, where their geography provides them a unique and strategic opportunity to live out their theology.

A competitive manifestation of the performing arts

Thus, sports are capable of creatively reflecting back to God his truth, beauty, and goodness through competitive performance.

An opportunity for worship

Thus, sports provide a specific opportunity to respond to displays of truth, beauty, and goodness by glorifying the Creator of the athlete(s) as the intricate creative Designer of fearfully and wonderfully made image bearers.

A testing ground that exposes character

Thus, sports place God's image bearers in the pressure of a limited and temporal arena, with the possibility of success or failure, in order to expose character with a view to cruciform Christian growth through discipline, thankfulness, sacrifice, and repentance.

An opportunity for witness

Thus, sports, like all of life, provide an outlet to glorify God and proclaim the gospel of Jesus Christ by pointing others to him; and in our cultural context, sports provide a strategic outlet where many lost people have a direct point of contact.

Helpful but not ultimate

Thus, sports must always be subordinate to God in Christ, a means and never an end.

Not one's source of identity

Thus, sports must never be the source of a Christian's identity, because Christ alone is the believer's identity, context, center, and end; so all other desires are subordinate to Christ. Nothing, including athletic failure, can steal the believer's contentment.

Notes

Introduction

1. Theodore Roosevelt, "Citizenship in a Republic," delivered at the Sorbonne in Paris, France, on April 23, 1910, http://www.theodore-roosevelt.com/images/research/speeches/maninthearena.pdf. Accessed June 5, 2015.

2. Theodore Roosevelt, "The Place of Athletics," *The Letters and Lessons of Theodore Roosevelt for His Sons,* ed. Doug Phillips (San Antonio, TX: Vision Forum, 2001), 35.

3. Jeanne Hess, *Sportuality: Finding Joy in the Games* (Bloomington, IN: Balboa Press, 2012), 98.

4. James Wagner, *Washington Post*, "Mark DeRosa Read Theodore Roosevelt Speech to Nationals before Game 4," October 11, 2012.

5. Roger Angell as quoted in Robert Elias, "A Fit for a Fractured Society: Baseball and the American Promise," *Baseball and the American Dream: Race, Class, Gender, and the National Pastime* (Oxford, UK: Routledge, 2001), 8.

6. Theodore Roosevelt, "At the Harvard Union," February 23, 1907, http://www.theodore-roosevelt.com/images/research/txtspeeches/240.txt. Accessed May 15, 2015.

Chapter One

1. Andy Crouch, *Culture Making: Recovering Our Creative Calling* (Grand Rapids, MI: InterVarsity, 2013), 23.

2. Andrew G. Fuller, *The Complete Works of Andrew Fuller: Expositions—Miscellaneous,* vol. 3, J. Belcher, ed. (Harrisonburg, VA: Sprinkle Publications, 1988), 8.

3. Duane A. Garrett, *Proverbs, Ecclesiastes, Song of Songs*, New American Commentary, vol. 14 (Nashville, TN: B&H Publishing Group, 1993), 220.

4. Kevin Clark, "Andrew Luck: The NFL's Most Perplexing Trash Talker," *Wall Street Journal*, December 16, 2014.

5. Charles Simeon, quoted by John Piper in *The Roots of Endurance* (Wheaton, IL: Crossway, 2002), 113.

Chapter Two

1. Darren Everson, "What the Rise of Southern Football Says about America," *Wall Street Journal*, December 5, 2008.

2. As quoted in Rick Bragg's "Down Here" (August 8, 2012), http://espn.go.com/college-football/story/_/id/8240383/rick-bragg-explains-history-traditions-south-obsession-football-espn-magazine. Accessed August 26, 2015.

3. Wayne Flynt, *Alabama in the Twentieth Century* (Tuscaloosa, AL: University of Alabama Press, 2006), 419.

4. William J. Baker, *Playing with God: Religion and Modern Sport* (Cambridge: Harvard Press, 2007), 106.

5. Wayne Flynt, *Keeping the Faith: Ordinary People, Extraordinary Lives* (Tuscaloosa, AL: University of Alabama Press, 2011), 215.

6. Malcolm Gladwell, "Offensive Play: How Different Are Dogfighting and Football?" *New Yorker,* October 19, 2009.

7. Roger I. Abrams, "A Gladiatorial Sport as National Pastime," *New York Times,* October 3, 2010.

8. Rodney Stark, *The Rise of Christianity* (San Francisco, CA: Harper, 1997), 214–15.

9. Rodney Stark, "A Double Take on Early Christianity: An Interview with Rodney Stark," *Touchstone Magazine* vol. 13, issue 1 (January/February 2000).

10. Louis R. Tarsitano, "Seriously Seeking Mysteries: Seekers, Liturgy, and Baseball," *Touchstone Magazine* vol. 16, issue 7 (September 2003).

11. Lesslie Newbigin, *Sign of the Kingdom* (Grand Rapids, MI: Eerdmans, 1981), 64.

12. As quoted in William Oddie, *Chesterton and the Romance of Orthodoxy: The Making of GKC 1874–1908* (Oxford: Oxford University Press, 2008), 150.

Chapter Three

1. Ralph Earle, "2 Timothy" *The Expositor's Bible Commentary*, ed. Frank E. Gaebelein, vol. 11 (Grand Rapids, MI: Zondervan, 1981), 399.

2. L. Ryken, J. Wilhoit, T. Longman, C. Duriez, D. Penney, and D. G. Reid, "Athletics," in *The Dictionary of Biblical Imagery* (Downers Grove, IL: InterVarsity, 2000), 54.

3. Craig S. Keener, *The IVP Bible Background Commentary: New Testament* (Downers Grove, IL: InterVarsity, 1993), 769.

4. Sal Paolantonio, *How Football Explains America* (Chicago, IL: Triumph Books, 2008), 110.

5. Ibid., 111.

6. John J. Miller, *The Big Scrum: How Teddy Roosevelt Saved Football* (New York, NY: Harper-Collins, 2011), 165.

7. Amos Alonzo Stagg, as quoted in William J. Baker, *Playing with God: Religion and Modern Sport* (Cambridge: Harvard University Press, 2007), 59.

8. R. J. Higgs, *God in the Stadium: Sports and Religion in America* (Lexington, KY: University of Kentucky Press, 1995), 92–93.

9. Ellis Lucia, *Mr. Football: Amos Alonzo Stagg* (New Jersey: A. S. Barnes and Co., 1970), 189.

10. Roger Angell, *The Summer Game* (Winnipeg, Canada: Bison Books, 2004), 41.

Chapter Four

1. Brad M. Griffin, "The Only Six Words Parents Need to Say to Their Kids About Sports—Or Any Performance," accessed from http://fulleryouthinstitute.org. Griffin responded graciously to my critique and said he understood my concerns and appreciated the interaction.

2. Diana Schaub, "America at Bat," *National Affairs* (Winter 2010), 115.

3. Doris Kearns Goodwin, *Wait Till Next Year* (New York, NY: Simon & Schuster, 1998), 1–2.

Chapter Five

1. Matthew Watkins, "Keller Football League's Nixing of Participation Trophies Fuels National Debate," *Dallas Morning News*, Metro, November 2013.

2. Eddie Brummelman, Sander Thomaes, Stefanie A. Nelemans, Bram Orobio de Castro, Geertjan Overbeek, and Brad J. Bushman, "Origins of Narcissism in Children," *Proceedings of the National Academy of Sciences* vol. 112, no. 12 (2015): 3659–662.

3. Anthony Esolen, "What Sports Illustrate," *Touchstone,* October 2003.

4. Scott Cacciola, "A Woman Among Boys," *New York Times*, August 20, 2014.

Chapter Six

1. Thomas Boswell, *Why Time Begins on Opening Day* (New York, NY: Penguin Books, 1984), 159.

2. A. Bartlett Giamatti, *Take Time for Paradise* (New York, NY: Bloomsbury, 1989), 71–91.

3. Peter Morris, *Catcher: The Evolution of an American Folk Hero* (Lanham, MD: Ivan R. Dee, 2009), 25–26.

4. Another exception being the lowering of the pitching mound in 1969.

5. Gilbert K. Chesterton, *Heretics/Orthodoxy* (Nashville, TN: Thomas Nelson, 2000), 247–48.

6. David Foster Wallace, "Federer as Religious Experience," *New York Times* (Aug. 20, 2006).

7. Malcolm Gladwell, "Offensive Play: How Different Are Dogfighting and Football?" *The New Yorker,* October 19, 2009. Since that piece, Gladwell has repeated similar assertions often.

8. Owen Strachan, "Our Shaken Faith in Football: Should Christian Fans Step Away from Such a Physically Devastating, Violent Sport?" *Christianity Today,* September 5, 2013, http://www.ctlibrary.com/ct/2013/september-web-only/our-shaken-faith-in-football.html.

9. Donald Wilhelm, *Theodore Roosevelt as an Undergraduate* (Boston, MA: John W. Luce and Company, 1910), 78–90.

10. Theodore Roosevelt, *The Strenuous Life: Essays and Addresses* (Mineola, NY: Dover, 2009), 158.

11. John J. Miller, *The Big Scrum: How Teddy Roosevelt Saved Football* (New York, NY: Harper Collins, 2011), 15.

12. James H. O'Keefe, Harshal R. Patil, Carl J. Lavie, Anthony Magalski, Robert A. Vogel, Peter A. McCullough, "Potential Adverse Cardiovascular Effects from Excessive Endurance Exercise," *Mayo Clinic Proceedings* vol. 87, issue 6 (June 2012): 587–95.

13. National Institute for Occupational Safety and Health (NIOSH) is a United States government research agency within the Centers for Disease Control and Prevention (CDC). "Heart Health Concerns for NFL Players," (2012), http://www.cdc.gov/niosh/pgms/worknotify/pdfs/NFL_Notification_01.pdf.

14. Bill Bradley, Interview with Daniel Flynn, "Author's 'War on Football' Sees Positive Aspects at All Levels of Life," http://www.nfl.com/news/story/0ap1000000243729/article/authors-war-on-football-sees-positive-aspects-at-all-levels. Accessed September 12, 2014.

15. Dale Robertson, "Youth Football Less Dangerous than Thought," *Houston Chronicle,* September 6, 2011.

16. National Center for Catastrophic Sport Injury Research, thirteenth annual report (1982–2012), http://nccsir.unc.edu/files/2014/06/NCCSIR-30th-Annual-All-Sport-Report-1982_2012.pdf.

17. Anthony Esolen, "What Sports Illustrate," *Touchstone,* October 2003.

18. C. S. Lewis, *The Screwtape Letters* (Nashville, TN: B&H Publishing Group, 1996), 104.

Chapter Seven

1. Urban Meyer speaking at 2012 Ohio High School Football Coaches Association Clinic.

2. Ibid.

3. Horatius Bonar, *Words to Winners of Souls* (Phillipsburg, NJ: P & R Publishing, 1995), 41.

4. Murray Polner, *Branch Rickey: A Biography* (Jefferson, NC: McFarland and Co., 2007), 186.

5. Arnold Rampersad, *Jackie Robinson: A Biography* (New York: Ballantine Books, 1998), 403.

6. Jackie Robinson, *Beyond Home Plate: Jackie Robinson on Life After Baseball*, ed. Michael G. Long (Syracuse, NY: Syracuse University Press, 2013), 9.

7. Jackie Robinson as told to Alfred Duckett, *I Never Had It Made* (New York, NY: GP Putnam's, 1972), 12.

8. Polner, *Branch Rickey*, 16.

9. Ibid., 19.

10. Lee Lowenfish, *Branch Rickey: Baseball's Ferocious Gentleman* (Lincoln, NE: University of Nebraska Press, 2007), 24.

11. Ibid., 11.

12. Wayne Stewart and Roger Kahn, *The Gigantic Book of Baseball Quotations* (New York, NY: Skyhorse Publishing, 2007), 59.

13. Branch Rickey, speech to the "One Hundred Percent Wrong Club," Jan. 20, 1956, Atlanta, GA, Branch Rickey Papers, Library of Congress, Washington, DC.

14. Doug Muzzio, CUNY TV Interview: City Talk: Jimmy Breslin, author, "Branch Rickey," April 8, 2011, https://www.youtube.com/watch?t=14&v=Vl9PKBwCTTw. Accessed April 4, 2014.

15. Robinson, *I Never Had It Made*, 32.

16. Polner, *Branch Rickey*, 4.

17. Jules Tygiel, *Baseball's Great Experiment: Jackie Robinson and His Legacy* (New York, NY: Oxford University Press, 1983), 48.

18. Hank Aaron with Lonnie Wheeler, *I Had a Hammer: The Hank Aaron Story* (New York, NY: HarperCollins, 1991), 19–20.

19. Lowenfish, *Branch Rickey*, 321.

20. Ibid., 2.

21. Polner, *Branch Rickey*, 253–54.

22. Peter Dreier, "The Real Story of Baseball's Integration that You Won't See in *42*," *The Atlantic* (April 11, 2013).

23. Lowenfish, *Branch Rickey*, 4.

24. John J. Montelone, ed., *Branch Rickey's Little Blue Book: Wit and Strategy from Baseball's Last Wise Man* (New York, NY: Macmillan, 1995), 108.

Conclusion

1. C. S. Lewis, *Mere Christianity* (New York, NY: Macmillan, 1952), 53–54.